"*The Sacred Gaze* is more than just an insightful overview of the relationship between healing and spirituality: it is a splendid general introduction to contemplative prayer. Susan R. Pitchford understands that contemplation is, at heart, a revolutionary way of viewing life, love, and God. With humility and grace, she explains the beauty and power of contemplative seeing, and how praying in this way can help you to become the authentic person God has created you to be."

—Carl McColman
Author of *Answering the Contemplative Call*
and *The Big Book of Christian Mysticism*

"*The Sacred Gaze* invites the reader to consider devoting the time and energy to cultivating the contemplative life, not only for its own sake, but also for the way deep experiences of God's unconditional love have the potential to bring a deeper level of healing to a wounded or spoiled identity. To experience oneself as beloved of God, expressed either through a mutual gazing in love upon one another in imaginative contemplation or as held in God's embrace in imageless prayer for long periods of time over a lifetime, leads to the discovery of one's true self that relieves one of the burden of all ego projects. To look into the mirror who is Christ is to discover one's own Christic identity."

—Dr. Janet Ruffing, RSM
Yale Divinity School
New Haven, Connecticut

The Sacred Gaze

Contemplation and the Healing of the Self

Susan R. Pitchford

Foreword by
Alan Jones

LITURGICAL PRESS
Collegeville, Minnesota
www.litpress.org

Cover design by Ann Blattner.

Christ, carving by Lars Christenson. Norwegian–American folk art from the Vesterheim Norwegian–American Museum in Decorah, Iowa. Photo by Gene Plaisted, OSC. © The Crosiers. Used with permission.

1 2 3 4 5 6 7 8 9

Library of Congress Cataloging-in-Publication Data

Pitchford, Susan.
The sacred gaze : contemplation and the healing of the self / Susan R. Pitchford.
pages cm
ISBN 978-0-8146-3568-1 — ISBN 978-0-8146-3593-3 (ebook)
1. Self-perception—Religious aspects—Catholic Church.
2. Contemplation. 3. Spirituality—Catholic Church. 4. Spiritual life—Catholic Church. 5. Healing—Religious aspects—Catholic Church. I. Title.

BV4598.25.P58 2014
248—dc23 2013045669

For Edie Burkhalter, who gives me permission
to be who I am.
And for Judith Gillette, a one woman oasis.

With all my love and gratitude.

Contents

Contents

Foreword

There's a *New Yorker* cartoon of a flashing sign on the highway which reads, "Welcome to Las Vegas: A faith-based community." There's no way of getting away from "faith"—a set of assumptions by which we approach and interpret life. How do we live in a world "addicted to velocity"? How do we resist the seductions of a culture that invites us to define ourselves by what we consume? Susan Pitchford has written a fiercely honest and probing "guide for the perplexed" which brings together sharp psychological insights with the ancient wisdom of the Christian spiritual tradition.

We live in an age in which there is no time for reflection, no time for catching up, no time for deepening, no time for wonder and amazement, no time for gathering up the scattered and mislaid bits and pieces which we call our life. On reading this remarkable book, I thought of Frederick Buechner's novel *Godric* in which he writes of the saint trying to recover those parts of himself he'd flung ahead of himself and of the parts he'd left behind.

The open secret of the spiritual life is that *contemplation* is at the center of a true understanding of humanity. Someone once defined contemplation as "a long loving look at the real." And that takes time. Contemplation isn't a one-way street. We not only contemplate but are the object of contemplation. We are gazed upon with love.

When I studied for the priesthood in an Anglican monastery, there was a painting of the crucifixion in the crypt chapel with the famous verse of John 3.16 ("God so love the world . . .") in Latin: "*Sic Deus dilexit mundum* . . ." which we translated as "God so *delighted* in the world . . ." I remember the prior leading us in a meditation inviting us to imagine God *delighting* in us. In fact, life (and especially the life of prayer) was the participation in the circle of delight—God delighting in us and us delighting in God and one another and the world.

Archbishop Rowan Williams writes, "As I see it, contemplation is the centre for our understanding of what the new humanity is. That is a humanity that is unconditionally receptive to God, unconditionally receptive to grace, and therefore profoundly open to what God is giving. Willing to live with the darkness and risk that that sometimes entails, conscious all the time of being anchored in the Son's contemplation of the Father, and the eternal mystery of the Trinity."

Susan Pitchford has outlined for us a great anthropological adventure, echoing Nicholas Berdyaev's famous phrase, "Man without God is no longer man" (forgive the non-inclusive language)—an adventure to heal the distorted and damaged sense of self. Something our world and our culture sorely needs. Pitchford writes, "Sometimes, when I am talking with a student about course work or their dreams and anxieties about the future, I'm struck by their completely unself-conscious radiance." That's it. This book is about the recovery of radiance—the sheer wonder and amazement of being alive and aware.

Alan Jones
Dean Emeritus
Grace Cathedral, San Francisco

Preface

If we desire to ascend to God, we must descend into our own humanity. The "descent" into himself or herself is not a preoccupation with the self and its concerns but the desire for God.

—Ilia Delio[1]

This book was born, as so many things are, out of a seeming coincidence. In my introductory sociology course I acquaint students new to the field with the characteristic ways in which sociologists think about social issues. We then spend the quarter practicing this way of thinking on a series of questions: Does the American education system promote equality of opportunity or hinder it? Why do some people embrace religions that seem bizarre to others? Why do some countries remain mired in poverty while others move forward? What factors create violent conflict between groups, and what are some steps they can take toward reconciliation?

These are interesting questions, but it occurred to me that my representation of the field to my students was skewed toward the "macro" or large-scale interaction end of the spectrum. Sociologists are also interested in interactions between individuals and small groups, so I started revising my course and added a new "micro" unit, one that would focus on self and identity. How do we become the people we are? What factors influence the content and meaning of our identities? Sociology tells us that the "self" is constructed through our interactions with others, whose responses mirror back to us the people we are. Of course, many sociologists, especially the theists among us, would argue that there is a core or essential self. Believing sociologists, like me, would say that the self is created and given by God. But all of us are interested, not only in the ways the self is shaped by society, but also in the ways we present ourselves to others.

While I was considering these things, I happened to be reading Ilia Delio's *Clare of Assisi: A Heart Full of Love*. This excellent book includes a fascinating chapter called "Image and Identity," which raises some of the same questions I'd been thinking about for my course. Two things occurred to me: first, maybe someone was trying to tell me something, and second, maybe what I was being told was that as a Christian, a Franciscan who loves Saint Clare, and a sociologist, I might be able to pull together insights from all of these sources to say something useful about self and identity.

There were two other reasons to consider taking on this project. One was that in my last book, *God in the Dark: Suffering and Desire in the Spiritual Life*, I had begun to talk about how greatly God desires to transform us, even transfigure us, so that we may be, as St. Peter suggested, "partakers of the divine nature."[2] I tried there to make the case that the darkest and driest times of life move us toward sharing in the glory of Christ, but I felt there was room to develop this idea further. The other, and probably the most compelling, reason came from my own experience. I once spoke to a group of fellow Franciscans about some hard times I'd been through years ago, and during the question-and-answer period afterward, someone asked me, "How did you heal after those experiences? How does a person come back from that?" I was taken off guard, and I remember shrugging and saying, "Time—and a lot of personal attention from Jesus."

I'm enough of a sociologist to know how dangerous it is to generalize from my own experience, which is why I've been careful in this book to say that God deals with each of us differently. But remembering the exchange in that session made me think that perhaps someone else could benefit from what I'd learned about personal healing. Like so many people, I have struggled with a battered sense of self, but I have learned from Teresa of Avila and others that a lot of good can come from spending time with Christ and "just looking at him."

So in this book, my goal is to draw some living water from three different sources: sociology, spirituality, and personal experience. The sociology in this book is hardly new, and it's not difficult to grasp. These are the kinds of basic ideas I share with college students, many of whom are three months away from high school. Yet there is some real insight there, particularly in Erving Goffman's famous dramaturgical perspective, which sees people as actors and looks at how we perform our selves for others. I'm also struck by how the early sociologist Charles Horton Cooley's idea of the "looking-glass self" (we learn who we are when our image is reflected back to us by others) ties into Clare of Assisi's advice to gaze into the mirror of the crucified Christ and there discover who we are. We cannot see ourselves without a mirror, but once we've found the One who can reflect our image back to us in both perfect truth and infinite love, I believe that gazing into that mirror holds the promise of healing.

As for my own experiences, they are offered for what they're worth. As Helen Keller is reputed to have said, "I am only one, but I am one." I am only one woman, and my experience will not be exactly like yours. God is not nearly as predictable as that. But I can tell you this: when I gaze into the mirror of Christ, what I see there is radically different from the self I thought I knew. To witness your own transfiguration, and to hear yourself called "Beloved," is a powerful thing. I am not suggesting in this book that contemplation alone can cure everything; if you've got a physical or mental illness, get the treatment you need. But I do believe that, although "gazing" will mean different things to different people (and we'll explore some of those differences as we go), what I am calling the "sacred gaze" is a potent source of healing. I invite you to explore it with me and ask the God who loves you, even more than you desire, to show you who you really are. I'm pretty sure the radiance you see reflected in that mirror will send you into a hard squint.

One final note, on the subject of language. Once again I am frustrated by the lack of gender-neutral pronouns in English, and by the way the alternatives grate on the ear. I just can't get used to repeating "God" several times in the course of a sentence ("God revealed Godself to God's people"). So while I've tried to mix it up occasionally, in general I've gone with masculine pronouns, not because God is more masculine than feminine, but because by virtue of being traditional, they seem to call less attention to themselves. I realize, however, that not everyone hears them this way, so my apologies to those who don't. One has to choose, but please feel free to mentally substitute the pronouns you prefer. Neither God nor I will mind.

Acknowledgments

It's said that fiction writers write the books they want to read. Perhaps nonfiction writers write the books they need to read; at least it seems I do. Once when I was about to get on a very long flight with a very bad back, I was grumbling to God about how it hurt, and why did I always have back flare-ups the day of travel, and where was he, and why wasn't he doing anything about it? And the still, small voice within me whispered, "Aren't you the author of *God in the Dark*?" The gentle reminder that I'd written a book on the presence of God in human suffering made me laugh, and we got across the Atlantic together on good terms.

In the present book I'm once again looking for answers to the most urgent questions in my own life, namely, who am I, and is God okay with that? Can I be? I don't think I'd have had the courage to write this book without the support of some of the wisest and dearest people in my life. First, Edie Burkhalter, TSSF, and Judith Gillette, TSSF, are sisters in the Third Order, Society of Saint Francis and continual reminders of how blessed I am to be part of that community. They both read the manuscript as I worked on it, and they both assured me that I wasn't the only one screwed up enough to need to read it. I'm deeply grateful also to Lev Raphael, whose friendship is a joy and whose generosity with the knowledge and experience gained from a long and prolific writing career is a Godsend. Teresa DiBiase, Obl. OSB, is another dear friend whose fingerprints are on this work. She read a draft when I was stuck and asked me one simple question that helped me find my way again. I'm indebted as well to Daniel Burkhalter, who though much younger than I is wise beyond my years and has taught me so much without obviously trying.

I also want to thank the two spiritual directors I've had during the course of this project: The Rev. Kathryn Ballinger and Laura Swan, OSB, both of whom have been like orienting stars in what is sometimes a pretty dark sky.

Once again my agent Kathleen Davis Niendorff has seen a project through from conception to completion. Without her generous help and kind encouragement all this stuff would just be an endless loop in my own head. I am also indebted again to the team at Liturgical Press: Hans Christoffersen, Lauren L. Murphy, and all the others have spent a lot of time and patience on me, and I hope the final product is worthy of their trust.

Finally, my own family deserve my deepest thanks, as they have dealt with me the longest and put up with the most. Nancy, Lynn, and Kim Pitchford; Bob Crutchfield; Danielle and Tally White: what would I be without you? You have given me so much joy.

Chapter 1

Radiant and Fully Alive

In Louisville, at the corner of Fourth and Walnut, in the center of the shopping district, I was suddenly overwhelmed with the realization that I loved all those people, that they were mine and I theirs, that we could not be alien to one another even though we were total strangers. It was like waking from a dream of separateness. . . . I have the immense joy of being . . . a member of a race in which God Himself became incarnate. As if the sorrows and stupidities of the human condition could overwhelm me, now that I realize what we all are. And if only everybody could realize this! But it cannot be explained. There is no way of telling people that they are all walking around shining like the sun.

—Thomas Merton[1]

Sometimes, when I am talking with a student about coursework or their dreams and anxieties about the future, I'm struck by their completely unself-conscious radiance. They are so young, so caught up in the pleasures and dramas and novelty of adulthood that they don't see what glorious beings they are, so full of potential, each one a whole world unto herself. But every now and then, I see. It's like witnessing a transfiguration, a vision of the human that lifts the veil and shows the divine image beneath. Saint Irenaeus, the second-century bishop of Lyons, said that "the glory of God is a human being fully alive." My young students are not yet fully alive, perhaps, but they have the wonder of human life within them. It dazzles me, and I lose my train of thought.

But Merton was right: there is no way of telling people that they're shining like the sun. I can only imagine their response if I tried to share the view of them that I've been graced to see. When the moment has passed, and I'm left alone with the impression still in my mind, I've wondered: What might someone, visited with the same graced vision, see in me? Is there a radiance in me too, if I could only see it?

It takes a considerable leap of faith for me to take this possibility seriously. Pride, as we know, is the deadliest of deadly sins, the one that fuels all the rest. But pride comes in two flavors: There are people whose pride takes the form of thinking excessively well of themselves. I've never really been one of them, though I can be pretty full of myself at times. The alternative is to become completely self-absorbed in continuous rumination on one's inadequacies, and that is much more my style. Shining like the sun? As Eliza says in *Pygmalion*: "Not bloody likely."

Yet growing older does have its consolations, the chief of which is growing up. If I woke up tomorrow and found myself twenty years old again, I'd find the nearest sharp object and kill myself with it. In the last decade or so, God has been working hard on my sense of self, replacing the wavy mirror in which I saw a distorted reflection with one that is straight and true. The image is radically changed: at first, I could see the odd sparkly bit, but in time I've come to see my own transfiguration take place. This is no flight of fancy; as St. Paul tells us, "All of us, gazing with unveiled face on the glory of the Lord, are being transformed into the same image from glory to glory, as from the Lord who is the Spirit."[2]

The key, I believe, is the *gaze*. God greatly desires to take our distorted sense of self—whether we value ourselves too little or too much—and restore to us our true identity. But this requires sustained, attentive looking into the mirror of God's providing. Many translations of St. Paul's text add that we are seeing the glory of the Lord *in a mirror*. Elsewhere, Paul says that we see "in a mirror, dimly, but then we will see face to face."[3] The face he means, of course, is God's own. Until that fullness comes, and we know as intimately as we are known, we see partially, in a mirror. But as we do, we are being transformed into the image and glory of Christ: a human being fully realized, fully alive.

The spiritual life is full of paradoxes, and one of them is that to see ourselves clearly, we need to look not toward ourselves but away. If we try to look directly at ourselves, we'll just look down at our own feet and fixate on how they're made of clay. A mirror gives us a truer image, and when Christ himself is our mirror, the reflection we'll see there can effect powerful healing of the self. But we must invest real time and energy gazing at it; there is no shortcut to this type of healing.

Why is God so committed to this healing, to helping us see ourselves as we really are? Because you can't approach God with a mask on. You're going to have to face him truthfully or not at all. And really, "not at all" is not an option, at least in the long run. Being "fully alive" means living authentically, not hiding from the truth about ourselves. God desires to turn back the tragedy of Eden, to make us naked and unashamed. But as the Christ-figure Aslan says in *The Lion, the Witch and the Wardrobe*, "This may be more difficult than you think." It's difficult because each of us has built up a false self, which we not only project to others but believe in wholeheartedly ourselves. In Thomas Merton's words:

> My false and private self is the one who wants to exist outside the reach of God's will and God's love—outside of reality and outside of life. And such a self cannot help but be an illusion. We are not very good at recognizing illusions, least of all the ones we cherish about ourselves. . . . All sin starts from the assumption that my false self, the self that exists only in my own

> egocentric desires, is the fundamental reality of life to which everything else in the universe is ordered.[4]

No one escapes from developing a false self, and our language about the self reflects this. The very word *person* is from the Latin *per sonare*, "to sound through." The idea is of a mask, through which an actor speaks.[5]

In his classic work *The Presentation of Self in Everyday Life*,[6] the sociologist Erving Goffman developed a theory of social interaction based on the metaphor of drama. Goffman examined the ways people perform their identity to audiences consisting of the others with whom they interact. Careful attention to costume, props, and how we deliver our lines are all meant to control how others see us; in Goffman's terms, the presentation of self is for the purpose of "impression management." It's not hard to see that this carefully staged self is likely to be more false than true, as our performances are geared to achieving our own objectives rather than God's. The false self is a persona we come to live in; we inhabit it like a house that gives us an artificial sense of safety, but it's built on sand and its structure is fundamentally unsound. Jesus warned that when the wind and rain come, houses built on lies will fall down and crush us.[7]

This is why he's so committed to dismantling our false self and restoring our true one. As the letter to the Ephesians puts it: "You were taught to put away your former way of life, your old self, corrupt and deluded by its lusts, and to be renewed in the spirit of your minds, and to clothe yourselves with the new self, created according to the likeness of God in true righteousness and holiness."[8] We not only are supposed to have a new self, but that self is supposed to be in "the likeness of God," righteous and holy, shining like the sun.

People often speak of "salvation" or "conversion" as if it were just a kind of "get out of jail free" card, an exemption from damnation. But God is not playing Monopoly; God is not playing at all. The Revelation given to John at Patmos makes it clear that nothing that loves and practices falsehood can be admitted to the presence of God.[9] Only what is true can stand in the presence of Truth. The truth of Jesus' identity was revealed to his closest friends in his transfiguration: "And he was transfigured before them, and his face shone like the sun, and his clothes became dazzling white."[10] Jesus didn't become someone different in that moment; the disciples simply saw the reality that had always been there. We are in a process of becoming Christlike, of being "transformed into the same image"; we are not there yet. But God, who lives in eternity, doesn't have to wait to see how we'll turn out. When God looks at us, he can see us transfigured, changed "from glory to glory." And if, through prayer, we are willing to enter that eternal reality with him, we can see this too.

What difference does it make? On a practical level, what changes when we come to see ourselves more and more as God sees us? I can't tell you exactly what difference that will make to you. But if I could go back fifteen years and tell my younger self what I've learned from this process, there are six lessons I'd pass on to the anxious, thirty-something me:

First, that thing you've done? God doesn't hate you for it. Second, those things that were done to you? God doesn't despise you for them. Guilt and shame do not have to come between you and God, or you and yourself.

Third, this is supposed to be a relationship. Cultivate it. This will take time, and there will be costs. Pay them. It's worth it.

Fourth, God desires to be in this relationship with you more than you can imagine or believe. You will just have to take that on faith. Fifth, if you could see yourself as God does, you'd do whatever it takes to grow into that identity. And you'd begin to see why it was worth it to him to suffer and die to restore and reclaim you.

Finally, you have a lot to learn about who God is too. The false images you've held of God are closely linked to the false images you've carried of yourself. They're both destructive. Lose them.

In practical terms, the most striking fruit of this process in my life has been peace—that deep, abiding peace that Jesus promised, which remains even during disappointment, failure, and grief. I no longer despair about the things in myself I cannot change, including my mortality. Having been on a flight that seemed to be going down over Dublin, with the two stout Irishmen in my row wetting themselves in fear, I can say with some assurance that I'm not afraid to die. At least, I wasn't that time. (My prayer on that occasion was, "Lord, I'd really like to see my family again. But in any case, I'd like to not see my lunch again.") I don't relish the prospect of losing others I'm close to, but I don't "grieve as others do who have no hope."[11] And I've seen that the more I live with the definition of myself that I've learned from God, the more I'm able to resist definitions imposed by others. This truer self is like a shield I can use to fend off attacks of negativity, both from without and within.

Don't misunderstand me: I remain as capable as ever of monumental blunders and daily screw-ups, and I'm still prone to fits of self-doubt and surges of ego. I haven't become any more organized or any more capable of feats of asceticism, large or small. I remain addicted to chocolate, and I still spend more on myself than a Franciscan probably should. But what I've learned from daily gazing into the mirror of Christ is that I don't have to wait till I've overcome all these things to be God's beloved. That is the reality right now, as surely as Jesus was divine before he dragged Peter, James, and John up the Mount of Transfiguration. That event didn't change Jesus. It just showed the disciples the truth of who he'd been all along, and that changed *them*. I am convinced that gazing into the mirror of Christ will change us too.

This book is a short course on how to see that you are in fact shining like the sun. I can tell you that you are, but only Christ can *show* you that you are. As the great Spanish mystic Teresa of Avila said to her sisters, "I'm not asking you to do anything more than *look at him*."[12] She knew, and I know, that he will take care of the rest.

Chapter 2

The Wounding of the Self

> *"I have been told so many lies," [Mack] admitted. Jesus looked at him and then with one arm pulled Mack in and hugged him. "I know, Mack, so have I. I just didn't believe them."*
>
> —William P. Young[1]

In the year 1253, Clare of Assisi wrote a letter to Agnes of Prague, a woman who, like Clare herself, had stepped away from wealth and privilege to give herself entirely to Christ. In this, her fourth and final letter to Agnes, Clare praises "Him whose beauty all the blessed hosts of heaven unceasingly admire." She refers to Christ by many names: "the Most High King," "the spotless Lamb," "the Lord of heaven and earth." But the most intriguing title Clare gives to Christ in this letter is "the mirror without blemish." "Gaze upon that mirror each day," she urges Agnes, ". . . and continually study your face within it."[2]

What was Agnes meant to see in this mirror? Clare directs her attention to Christ's poor and humble birth, his hard life, and, finally, "the *ineffable charity* that led Him to suffer on the wood of the Cross and to die there the most shameful kind of death."[3] As the life of the poor Crucified unfolds under her gaze, Clare understands that the cross represents the unfathomable depths of God's love. To empty himself of his divine rights and take on the status of a slave so that he could obey to the point of death on a cross[4] was an act of unspeakable, ineffable love. Agnes was to understand that this love was directed not just at the world but at her personally.

But there was something else Clare wanted Agnes to see. "Gaze upon that mirror each day, *O Queen and Spouse of Jesus Christ*, and continually study your face within it."[5] Gazing into the mirror of Christ's sacrifice would reveal to Agnes her own true identity: noble, royal, honored, and beloved. This young woman who had declined the hand of the Holy Roman Emperor and disappeared into cloistered obscurity was to gaze on the mirror of Christ and find her own face, her own self, revealed: transformed, transfigured, lit by the uncreated Light into a shocking and unsuspected beauty. Whatever the world and her own dark voices might say about her, this was the truth, this she could know for sure. In other words, Clare was inviting Agnes into contemplation.

The Looking-Glass Self

As a sociologist, I know that I cannot know my "self" directly any more than I can know my physical appearance without a mirror. I come to know my self, the sort of person I am, as others reflect that self to me. If they're interested in my ideas, that suggests that I'm smart; if they laugh at my jokes, I'm probably funny; and if they line up to ask me out, I can guess that I'm attractive. The reverse is also true: the responses of others can tell me that I'm unattractive, slow-witted, and socially awkward. Over a hundred years ago, sociologist Charles Horton Cooley wrote of the "looking-glass self," the idea that we discover who we are through our interactions with others, who serve as a mirror for us:

Each to each a looking-glass
Reflects the other that doth pass.[6]

If Cooley was a pretty regrettable poet, he was a good sociologist. Those of us in the field today take it for granted that the self is known and even constructed through interaction. We are inherently relational: each of us is embedded in a web of social relationships, and our ties to others in our networks shape our lives, our choices, and the people we become.

Cooley would have made a good theologian too. Of course, I don't know that he actually believed in God. But those who do, and who spend a lot of time trying to figure out what God is up to, also tell us that the self is inherently relational. We learn from Genesis that we are made in God's image; that is, in our very nature, we resemble God. The doctrine of the Trinity tells us that the nature of God is loving relationship. "God is love," says John's letter,[7] and the twelfth-century mystical theologian Richard of St. Victor had a useful explanation of the "relationship" part: A God who exists from eternity but is unitary cannot be "love," because there's no one else around to receive that love. And even humans, once created, would not have the capacity to receive the fullness of God's perfect love. A God in two persons has an Other to love, but a deep love between two can be exclusive, self-absorbed, a closed system. When a third is added, Richard argued, the love becomes open, a circle that invites others in.[8] A triad is the most difficult of relationships to keep in balance, as many an embittered lover can attest. But I'm sure there's a lot less drama and hard feelings when you're divine and your very nature is perfect love.

Christianity teaches that humans are created in the image of this triune God, and one way we mirror that "threeness" is by being enmeshed in a threefold network of loving relationships: we love God, we love our neighbor, and we love ourselves. This is our identity, and this is why our nature and purpose, our ideal life, can be summed up in the two great commandments: love

God with all you have and all you are, and love your neighbor as yourself.[9] This, Jesus said, is the whole point of our existence, "all the law and the prophets." This is who we really are, and all the instruction manuals were given to bring us to the fulfillment of this identity.

Perhaps you've spotted the snag here. You don't have to be a theologian to realize that we humans love God with considerably less than all our heart, soul, mind, and strength, and as for our neighbors, we mostly love them about as badly as we love ourselves. Our tradition explains this to us too. Whether you prefer to speak of "original sin" or, with Lady Julian, of "original wounds,"[10] there is a deep-seated kink to our nature. Something has gone badly wrong, and with St. Paul, we continually fail to do the things we want while repeatedly doing the things we hate.[11] You may disagree with Thomas Cranmer's diagnosis that "there is no health in us."[12] But it's hard to argue that there isn't a whole lot of room for improvement.

The False Self

Our failure to love as we should has all kinds of consequences, of which I'm convinced we'll get a full reckoning one day. Surely there will come a time when we'll have to grow up at last and face the reality of our lives and our choices. In the meantime, however, one of the most disastrous consequences of our lack of love is to our identity itself. Precisely because we resist growing up and out of the self-centeredness that we needed to survive as infants, we construct a *false self*, which the Trappist monk and teacher of centering prayer Thomas Keating calls "the root cause of human misery."[13] The false self is born when we fail to move out of the stage in which the infant must believe he is the center of the universe. By four years of age, Keating says, we're building

> programs for happiness that identify with the symbols in the culture that express security, power, affection, and esteem. When these are frustrated . . . off go the afflictive emotions: shame,

> humiliation, grief, sorrow, discouragement, fear. These afflictive emotions can become so painful that we repress some of them into the unconscious where the energy remains and opposes the free flow of natural energies and the energy of grace. Paul calls this stage "the old man."[14]

The false self knows no moderation: either I am the center of the universe or, as I have heard the alternative put, I am the piece of garbage at the center of the universe. Either I am a pretty good person whom others should attend to and emulate, or I am the "chief of sinners,"[15] and no one has ever disappointed God as spectacularly as I. It's either pride or self-contempt, which, as I've suggested, is really just the shadow side of pride. For those of us whose deadliest sin is self-contempt, we know the "afflictive emotions" it brings: the shame, the discouragement, and the deep sense of ugliness and inadequacy. Whatever form the false self takes, it is an illusion; it is a lie.

Jesus had the compassion and the honesty to tell us that this self is going to have to die if we are going to live authentically.[16] This is the paschal mystery: nothing that has not died can live forever. If our perfection can only be achieved when we've grown up and faced the reality of our lives and our choices, then the false self represents a flight from reality and a prolongation of spiritual infancy. It is the illusion of autonomy, of self-sufficiency, of centrality, whether that feels good or terrible. Illusions can be comfortable, or they can be oppressive, but it's the truth that sets us free.[17]

This is why Jesus taught us that we must be born all over again. As Thomas Merton said, "To be born again is not to become somebody different, but to become ourselves."[18] The false self is a liar; it distorts who we are. It promises that happiness and fulfillment lie in the recognition of our talents, the advancement of our agendas, and the pursuit of our interests. Most people aren't in a position to test these promises thoroughly, because life doesn't give us the opportunity to see what "having it all" feels like. In the media, though, we are treated day after day to the spectacle of self-destruction among those who do have it all and discover that the false self is a compulsive liar.

The Self under Assault

The consolation to those of us who aren't rich and famous is that at least we don't have to have our afflictive emotional meltdowns on the cover of *People* magazine. But that doesn't make the frustration of our false self, and the consequent feelings of shame, inadequacy, and despair, any less real. Consider the effect of having a very narrow (and for most of us, unattainable) range of body shapes and looks socially defined as desirable. An important study by sociologist Melissa Milkie showed that even if we personally reject these images as unrealistic and dismiss them as unimportant, they can still have a lot of power over our self-image if we believe that others who matter to us do buy into them.[19] Some people's sense of self is so ravaged by these social definitions that they can't even see themselves accurately *with* a mirror. They call this "body dysmorphic disorder," and suicide rates among its victims are forty-five times higher than those of the general population.[20] That doesn't count the slow suicides accomplished through eating disorders or the deaths from complications of cosmetic procedures.

Our identities are under assault on every side. I'm astonished at the number of young people, some of them barely into their teens, who have committed suicide as a result of being bullied by their peers, usually because they were defined as "different" somehow. Ryan Halligan, who had trouble keeping up academically, was tormented by a group of kids from the time he was in fifth grade through middle school. In the last episode of many, he was tricked into confiding in a girl he liked who publicly denounced him as a "loser." He committed suicide at age thirteen.[21] In a similar case, Megan Meier was a girl who suffered from attention deficit disorder, depression, and self-loathing because of her weight. She was subjected to cyber-bullying by a former friend and the friend's mother, who opened a fake MySpace account under the name "Josh Evans." Megan confided in "Josh," and the woman and her daughter used her messages to publicly humiliate her. She hanged herself just before her fourteenth birthday.[22]

Technology is offering us creative new ways to destroy each other and ourselves. Both eighteen-year-old Jesse Logan and thirteen-year-old Hope Witsell killed themselves after sexually explicit photos they'd sent to boyfriends were made public. After months of being taunted as a "slut" and a "whore," Hope knotted a pink scarf around the canopy of her bed and strangled herself.[23] A pink scarf and a canopied bed—could anything say "innocent girlhood" more clearly? And yet, these were the means a girl named Hope used to escape from an identity she believed to be fractured beyond repair.

These are dramatic cases, but how many of us grind through each day laboring under the burden of not being attractive enough, smart enough, successful enough, stable enough, or sober enough to be at peace in our own skins? These doubts can be especially agonizing when they attack an otherwise strong sense of self-confidence; they are like a worrying ding in the windshield. God knows, many of my academic colleagues seem blessed with an abundance of what you could charitably call self-confidence. Yet I know that it's not uncommon for scholars to harbor a secret fear that they will someday be unmasked, revealed as frauds who lack the expertise they're supposed to have. This can take on comical forms, like the dream in which someone figures out that because of some technicality, you never finished the third grade. This means that every academic achievement since—up to and including your PhD—is revoked, and you're going to have to quit your job at the university, give back all that grant money, and get a gig at McDonald's.

A very serious academic burden is borne by minority students who are strong academically but who face added pressure to perform because of stereotypes that set up expectations of failure. These students are dealing not only with the false selves they've created, as we all do, but also with what you might call a "collective false self," created for them by a hostile and disparaging culture. Social psychologist Claude Steele's work has shown that these negative group images, and the expectations and anxiety they arouse, can create a self-fulfilling prophecy that sets bright and talented people up to underperform. When this cycle is repeated often enough, it tells the person that school is not a safe place to invest her energy, because it will not be rewarded. This can ultimately lead to disengagement with school, and another promising career ends up stillborn.[24]

Returning to the individual level, the sociology of crime and deviance highlights another way in which social processes can generate assaults to our identity. According to labeling theory,[25] there are two kinds of deviant behavior: primary deviance and secondary deviance. Primary deviance consists of the norm violations we all commit at one time or another: exceeding the speed limit, underage drinking, or showing up for an occasion over- or underdressed. Most of us get away with these things and survive with our identities more or less intact.

But sometimes we don't. Sometimes other people react so negatively to a person's behavior that he is publicly labeled "deviant": an alcoholic, a pervert, a criminal. This labeling shapes the person's identity in a way that becomes a self-fulfilling prophecy: if I've been labeled a "delinquent," then rather than resist that identity, I may figure I now have nothing to lose and start hanging out and identifying with the other delinquent kids, doing the things they do. Those delinquent acts, which arise from the labeling itself, constitute secondary deviance.

Labeling theorists point out that we are not all equally vulnerable to labeling processes, nor are we equal in our ability to impose labels on others. It's a question of power. Criminal justice authorities, for example, have considerable power to impose labels on kids and adults, and non-white and poor people have little power to shake those labels off. Someone whose personal or group traits or behaviors are strongly rejected by others has been stigmatized; in Erving Goffman's terms, that person's identity has been "spoiled."[26]

Clearly, some of our "selves" are more wounded than others, and some of us heal more readily than others. But none of us escapes this struggle without scars, however carefully they may be concealed. So we grieve because we're getting older, or we grieve for those who never had the chance to get old. We grieve because we fear childbearing wreaked such havoc on our bodies that we're no longer attractive to our mate, or we grieve because we can't bear children. Our careers haven't turned out the way we hoped, or they have, and we're wondering if that's all there is. We wanted to change the world, and instead we're living lives of quiet desperation, or just bland respectability. Or everything has gone as we'd hoped it would, but we know that all it takes is a diagnosis or a mistake on the freeway to bring it all down around our ears.

At one level, none of this is new. Human nature and the human condition don't change much, and there have always been people who built themselves up by making others small. Jesus' story of the Pharisee and the tax collector tells us that the pattern goes back at least two thousand years. The religious leader thanks God that he's better than this outcast scum who, for his part, doesn't dare to raise his eyes toward heaven but stares at the ground and begs God for mercy. He, at least, was praying honestly; if he'd let his false self take charge, he would probably have considered himself beyond the bounds of mercy and given up, as Judas did. The story of the competition between Abraham's wife Sarah and the servant Hagar shows that envy and rivalries go back almost another two thousand years. We can probably assume they've been with us from the beginning.

Social Change and the Search for the Self

Some things have changed, though. As we saw earlier, technology and the mass media make it possible to spread widely and rapidly both the standards to which we hold people and their failure to measure up to them. Additionally, the move from homogeneous, close-knit, traditional communities to multicultural, urban, industrial, and postindustrial society (which sociologists characterize as the shift from *gemeinschaft* to *gesellschaft*) has brought with it an extreme individualism. Our identities, once defined by the tribe, are now our own to construct, and when we fall, we go down alone.[27]

These forces were already in motion in St. Clare's day: urbanization, a rising middle class that was displacing the old nobility (into which Clare had been born), and a widening gap between haves and have-nots were creating a lot of unrest in her time. Much of this unrest was manifested in new religious movements. Some, like the Cathars, were considered heretical; some, such as the Beguines, were essentially orthodox but viewed with suspicion; still others, like the mendicant orders (Dominicans and Franciscans), were strictly orthodox—so strictly that they later served as principal agents of the Inquisition. Nobody's perfect.

Times of upheaval do seem to generate new religious movements, and this was as true in thirteenth-century Europe as it was in 1960s America.[28] These are times of uncertainty, when the old answers no longer seem to be working, and people search for new ones. When Clare went looking for her answers, she teamed up with Francis of Assisi to cofound the Franciscan movement. The church being what it was, Francis got approval for his new way of life almost immediately, while Clare had to fight to her dying breath for the Rule she'd devised for her community. The church spent years trying to make Clare into a Benedictine; this would mean holding communal property rather than living with what Clare called the "privilege of poverty," which would force her community to rely every day on God's provision alone.

Because she lived in a time of social upheaval, Clare was pushed back to the fundamental question of her own identity. Who was she to be, and how was she to live in the world? The church kept pressing her to accept the old answers and the old way of life those answers implied. The Benedictine way is a good way and, because of its values of moderation and balance, proved to be more sustainable in the long run than the extreme paths originally chosen by Francis and Clare. But Clare resisted this for herself because of her deep sense of who she was and the way to which she was called; for her, being the bride of Christ meant she had committed herself to one Spouse and was not going to accept gifts from his rivals. It was out of that settled conviction that she was able to resist Rome itself and forge an entirely new way of life for religious women. And it was in the mirror of the Crucified that Clare came to know exactly who she was, and Whose she was.

Francis too grappled with these questions. Early in his life, he had to decide whether he was to be one of the *majores*, the upwardly mobile merchant class into which his successful father had raised the family. With little interest in his father's business, Francis tried on the role of soldier, thinking that "knight" would be an identity he could assume with pleasure. Eventually, his conversion led him and his followers to adopt the counter-cultural identity of *minores*, the lesser ones, the small ones, the downwardly mobile. It's interesting to me, though, that this does not seem to have settled the matter for Francis, who was still asking the identity question at the climactic moment of an intensely spiritual life.[29] Tradition has it that about two years before his death, Francis was praying at a secluded hermitage on Monte Alverna when he had a vision in which a six-winged seraph engraved in his flesh the wounds of Christ's passion. Francis had been praying, "My God and my all, who are you, my sweetest Lord and God; and who am I, a poor little worm, your servant?"[30]

Who am I? Francis had renounced wealth and privilege, had lost family and respectability, and had founded a successful new religious order only to lose that too. A saint by public acclamation, his leadership rejected by his own community, his health in ruins, all worldly ambition long since abandoned, and spiritually in crisis, Francis asks, *Who am I?* The stigmata are God's answer: "You are *alter Christus*, 'another Christ,' so closely conformed to My Son that your body itself is united with his passion." When Francis looked into the mirror of the Crucified, this is what he saw: no false self, neither exaggerated vices nor inflated virtues, just the simple, staggering truth of his union with Christ.

Into the Looking Glass

And what about us? What would we see in that mirror? We likely have some idea of the world's answer to the question, "Who am I?" We see its answers reflected in the individuals with whom we interact and in the socially defined expectations conveyed to us through the media and other channels. And we know our own inventory of answers, from which we may draw different selections depending on how a given day is going. But the fact that the phrase "Does this make my butt look big?" has become a standing cultural joke suggests our deep uncertainty about how others see us and how well we conform to social norms. We know it's all in the eye of the beholder. We just aren't sure which beholders' eyes we can trust.

What we all need is someone who sees clearly and will speak the truth to us in love. Clare knew where to find that: "Gaze upon that mirror each day . . . and continually study your face within it." If, as sociology tells us, we come to know who we are through interaction with others in our networks, then we need to spend a lot of time interacting with the only One in our network who sees us with complete clarity and perfect charity and is committed to our transformation into his faithful, untarnished image.

This is why the *gaze* is so essential. If I want a true answer to the question "Who am I?" I must stop looking at those who will give me false answers. The world around us and the false self within us are a funhouse whose mirrors only show us distortions. We need to tear ourselves away from those distorted images, fascinating as they can be, and take ourselves to the quiet place where we can gaze into the true Mirror without interruption and without distraction. Francis found his answer in the solitude of Alverna; Clare found hers in the seclusion of the cloister. She invited Agnes into contemplation precisely because it is the contemplative gaze into the face of Christ that gives us the truest knowledge, and the deepest healing, of who we are.

It may take us time to accept it, but the more we devote ourselves to that sacred gaze, the more the authentic self will displace the false self and the more our true self will be transformed into the image of God's own beloved Son.[31] This is the truth that will set us free from the deceptive programs of self-fulfillment based on the gratification of our own ego. And this is where we will find the deep, circumstance-defying, and incomprehensible peace that Jesus promised.[32]

In the pages ahead, we will explore the healing power of the contemplative gaze and some practical suggestions for how to enter into contemplative prayer and find that healing. It is clear from Jesus' teachings, his ministry of healing, and his passion that he deeply desires our restoration to wholeness. There are many means through which this restoration occurs, including everything from therapy to active service to the humblest members of his family, but contemplating the face of Christ is perhaps the most direct and intensive form of healing. Further, as I have mentioned elsewhere,[33] the gaze at Christ motivates service to others, because after staring into that light, you keep seeing and loving it everywhere you look.

I hope that these pages will help you move closer to the peace, freedom, and wholeness God desires for you. It may seem a bit self-indulgent to practice a spiritual discipline for the sake of finding one's self, a little reminiscent of the excesses of the "Me generation." But this is another deception; we are following

Clare here, not Narcissus. A whole self is not an end in itself, because the self is relational. We seek healing of our self for the healing of our relationships, both vertical and horizontal, and even—each of us in our small way—for the healing of the world. Trying to serve others from the false self is building on sand, and Jesus warned us about that. Let us allow him to show us a more excellent way.

Chapter 3

The Healing of the Self: Does God Care?

> *The great spiritual teachers tell us that when the Divine Life is born in us, that which is false and illusory begins to die. This is promising and it is frightening. No one can face that unless he or she is pretty sure that beneath that which is unreal there is a deeper and better reality. When we start to trust our own best experience of God, the One who says "Have no fear," and "I am with you always," that deeper reality begins to come forth.*
>
> —John P. Gorsuch[1]

Let me start by admitting that it can be hard at times to believe that God has any great desire to heal. Most of the sociology courses I teach revolve around various forms of human suffering: racism, poverty, disease, slavery, and genocide. I think I can understand why many people, if they believe in God at all, think that a God with all that power could be doing a bit more to deal with the human condition. Or perhaps they see God acting, but that action seems capricious: one person's goldfish recovers from the goldfish plague while another person's child dies of cancer. What can God be thinking?

As long as people have been looking toward God, they've been asking this question. The book of Job, which is probably the oldest book in the Bible, revolves around the puzzle of why God allows apparently decent people to suffer. And you'd think that if they were going to have a whole book in the Bible dedicated to this question, it would have the answer, wouldn't you? But it doesn't, really. Job asks the question, but God answers with questions of his own: "Where were you when I laid the foundation of the earth? Tell me, if you have understanding."[2] Essentially the answer is, "You with the tiny brain: Shut up." Or, in the rather more elegant language of Ecclesiastes, "God is in heaven, and you upon earth; therefore let your words be few."[3] (The fact that this book doesn't end here shows that I have not yet taken that advice to heart.)

In all of theology there is not a tougher question than the problem of evil; that is, why does a God who is all good, all knowing, and all powerful allow suffering? If God is so good, then he must want to relieve suffering; if he doesn't, it must mean that he doesn't know about it (he isn't all knowing) or else he isn't able to (he's not all powerful). I have addressed this problem elsewhere;[4] others[5] have done it better in their own books. The answer I find most satisfying is that God gave humans the dignity of free will, because we could not truly love him or each other without freedom; there is no such thing as forced love. But we have used that freedom to make destructive choices, and until the consequences of those choices are fully played out and the process of healing complete, we and all of creation suffer—the righteous along with the unrighteous, the just with the unjust.[6]

But all answers to the question are ultimately unsatisfying, unless you're prepared to take a certain number of things on faith. These would include, among others, the idea that our timeline and God's do not coincide,[7] that a greater purpose will ultimately put the present sufferings into a perspective that will make sense,[8] and that finite human minds do, indeed, need to take certain things about the Infinite on faith. For Christians, the life of Christ tells us that, whatever questions may remain, of this we can be certain: God is not indifferent to our suffering. He was born into poverty, spent much of his public ministry relieving people's misery, and ended by answering our cries with his own blood.

I'm not going to try to disentangle the problem of evil here, but I do want to address one specific question: Assuming that God does care about our predicament, why should the healing of our *identity* be a particularly high priority? Of all the things about us that God could deal with—how we treat each other, how we care for the earth, even what we believe about him/her—is there any reason to think that the question of identity is especially important in God's eyes? I believe there is, and that some of the most powerful reasons for believing this come from Scripture, so let's begin there.

The Importance of Jesus' Identity

The case has been made[9] that the matter of Jesus' identity is the central question of the gospels, standing like a fulcrum on which the rest turns. Unlike the historic creeds of the church, the gospels don't tell us what to believe about Jesus. Instead, they narrate his story and invite the reader to answer Jesus' question: "Who do you say that I am?" It's a question the various characters in the gospels ask, over and over. Jesus forgives the woman weeping at his feet, and the other dinner guests ask, "Who is this who even forgives sins?"[10] Jesus calms a storm, and his disciples ask each other, "Who then is this, that even the wind and the sea obey him?"[11] A nervous King Herod, learning of Jesus' growing fame, wonders, "John I beheaded; but who is this about whom I hear such things?"[12] By the time of Jesus' final entry into the holy city, everyone is asking the same question: "When he entered Jerusalem, the whole city was in turmoil, asking, 'Who is this?'"

The times when this question receives an authoritative answer are the pivotal moments of the gospel narratives (apart from the resurrection itself, which is the definitive answer). At Jesus' baptism, a voice speaks from heaven: "This is my Son, the Beloved, with whom I am well pleased."[13] It's significant that, virtually as soon as this declaration is made, Jesus is tempted to doubt it. Jesus goes directly from his baptism to the wilderness, where he fasts and struggles for forty days and nights. Matthew's gospel tells us that the devil comes to him when he's vulnerable and says, "*If* you are the Son of God, command these stones to become loaves of bread. . . . *If* you are the Son of God, throw yourself down [from the pinnacle of the temple]."[14] Finally, the tempter offers Jesus "all the kingdoms of the world and their splendour"[15] if Jesus will fall down and worship him—that is, if Jesus will deny his own identity and perpetrate a lie by inverting their true positions and ascribing divinity to the evil one. Jesus invites the devil to go to hell, because even at his weakest, he will not assume an identity that is not true.

Again, at the transfiguration, the voice from the cloud declares, "This is my Son, the Beloved; listen to him!"[16] Notice once again how quickly afterward Jesus is face-to-face with the demonic in the form of a spirit that has taken hold of a boy. The disciples have been trying to exorcise the child, without success, and you can almost hear the weariness in Jesus' voice: "You faithless generation, how much longer must I be among you? How much longer must I put up with you? Bring him to me."[17]

We get the impression that there was a cosmic struggle over Jesus' true identity, in which he had to maintain his sense of self "against," as the letter to the Ephesians puts it, "principalities, against powers . . . against spiritual wickedness in high places."[18] But the struggle was also against earthly powers. The raising of Lazarus from the dead was one of Jesus' most spectacular miracles and one that put them both in serious danger. Before calling Lazarus from the tomb, Jesus wept, and then he prayed, "Father, I thank you for having heard me. I know that you always hear me, but I have said this for the sake of the crowd standing here, so that they may believe that you sent me."[19] As a result of this miracle, the authorities sought to kill both Jesus and Lazarus.[20] Jesus must have known the risk he was taking, but his prayer suggests that the consequences would be worth it if the people would finally understand who he was.

Of course, it was Jesus' closest friends whom he most desired to get his identity right. When Jesus asked the disciples point-blank who they believed him to be, Peter had the right answer: "You are the Messiah, the Son of the living God."[21] Jesus blessed him and used that moment to redefine Peter's own identity, giving him both a new name and a new call: "Blessed are you, Simon son of Jonah! . . . And I tell you, you are Peter, and on this rock I will build my church, and . . . I will give you the keys of the kingdom of heaven."[22] A week or so later, Peter, along with James and John, would witness the transfiguration, in which Jesus' identity as the "Son of the Living God" was made vividly, even frighteningly, clear.[23] "I'll believe it when I see it" is not how it works in matters of the spirit—rather, the other way around.

In John's gospel, we see again how vitally important it was to Jesus that people answer the question about his identity correctly. Jesus presses the issue with a series of "I am" statements, echoing the name by which Israel had known their God since the days of Moses: "I am that I am," or "I am that am."[24] Notice that God chose to be known through a statement of identity, of pure being, rather than a name that would emphasize God's actions or roles; it's *I am*, not *I do*, *I say*, or even *I command*.

To appreciate the significance of Jesus' "I am" statements, it's essential to understand the importance of names in Jewish thought. A name is not just a matter of taste or of combining nice sounds: "The name conveys the nature and essence of the thing named. It represents the history and reputation of the being named."[25] So when Moses asks God for his name, "Moses is not asking 'what should I call you;' rather, he is asking 'who are you; what are you like; what have you done.' That is clear from God's response. God replies that He is eternal, that He is the God of our ancestors, that He has seen our affliction and will redeem us from bondage."[26] God's people were taught to treat his name with the utmost seriousness and devotion. Devout Jews do not casually write the name of God, lest it be defaced or erased, and the four-letter Name is not to be spoken aloud; other names are pronounced in its stead, including simply Ha-Shem ("the Name"). Although this prohibition does not date back to the beginnings of Israel, it was in effect by the time of Jesus, and there was never a time in Jewish history when the sanctity of God's name was not observed.[27]

So when Jesus goes around saying, "*I am* the light of the world,"[28] "*I am* the gate for the sheep,"[29] "*I am* the bread of life,"[30] he is not just conjugating the verb *to be* as I do when I say "I am a writer," "I am a sociologist," or "I am from Seattle." He is saying at the most profound level who he is, what he is like, and what he is doing, and he's speaking with ultimate authority. When the crowd begins to sense this, they ask him, "What must we do to perform the works of God?" You can almost hear their thought process: "Here is someone who can cut through all of our confusion and tell us what really matters." Jesus answers, "This is the work of God, that you believe in him whom he has sent."[31] Just get my identity right, he says, and God will be pleased.

As Jesus nears the end, his identity statements to his friends seem to grow more urgent: "I am the resurrection and the life," he says to the grieving Martha; "Do you believe this?"[32] Reassuring his disciples before he leaves them, Jesus tells them, "I am the way, and the truth, and the life,"[33] and, "I am the true vine . . . abide in me."[34] In public, especially in confrontations with the religious authorities, he becomes increasingly pointed, forcing them to a choice: "You will die in your sins unless you believe that *I am*."[35] Although this passage is often rendered "unless you believe that I am he," the original Greek does not include the word "he," and adding it tends to obscure the fact that Jesus is making a direct claim to divinity here, infuriating his listeners. He will repeat that claim even more explicitly a few verses later: "Very truly, I tell you, before Abraham was, *I am*."[36] His opponents certainly understood the claim he was making; they prepared to stone him for blasphemy, but he slipped away.

When Jesus finally goes on trial before Pilate, it's the same questions again: Who are you? Where are you from? Are you the king of the Jews? Phillip Cary points out[37] that, paradoxically, it's Pilate who's on trial here, though he doesn't know it. Jesus, ever in control in John's gospel, renders a verdict: "the one who handed me over to you is guilty of a greater sin."[38] It is always Jesus who judges, and his judgment is based on our answer to that central question, Who do *you* say that I am?

I've gone on at some length about the centrality of Jesus' identity in the gospels to make the point that how people understood his identity mattered deeply to Jesus. The church went on to spend the first few centuries of its history trying to get this right. In Christianity, as in Judaism, the question of first importance concerns the identity and nature of God. But the next question to be answered is, "Who are we in relation to God?" Israel had its answer: they were the people of the covenant, chosen by God to be "a light to the nations."[39]

The Importance to Jesus of Our Identity

For Christians, I think it's fair to turn Jesus' question around and ask, as St. Francis did on Alverna, "Who do *You* say that *I* am?" Francis insisted that "what a man is before God, that he is and nothing more." So it's crucial that we know who we are before God—not who we are in the distorted images reflected to us by the media, popular culture, and the people in our lives, whether they wish us well or ill. It is what we see in the mirror that is Christ that matters. And if God's identity is of the utmost importance, and we are made in that divine image, then who we are matters too.

We see this affirmed in much of Jesus' healing ministry, but it is especially vivid in his encounter with the Gerasene demoniac, which appears in all three Synoptic Gospels.[40] It's an identity story, in that Jesus encounters a broken identity and dramatically, compassionately, restores it. Let's look at Luke's rendition:

> *Then they arrived at the country of the Gerasenes, which is opposite Galilee. As he stepped out on land, a man of the city who had demons met him. For a long time he had worn no clothes, and he did not live in a house but in the tombs. When he saw Jesus, he fell down before him and shouted at the top of his voice, "What have you to do with me, Jesus, Son of the Most High God? I beg you, do not torment me"—for Jesus had commanded the unclean spirit to come out of the man. (For many times it had seized him; he was kept under guard and bound with chains and shackles, but he would break the bonds and be driven by the demon into the wilds.) Jesus then asked him, "What is your name?" He said, "Legion"; for many demons had entered him. They begged him not to order them to go back into the abyss.*
>
> *Now there on the hillside a large herd of swine was feeding; and the demons begged Jesus to let them enter these. So he gave them permission. Then the demons came out of the man and entered the swine, and the herd rushed down the steep bank into the lake and was drowned.*
>
> *When the swineherds saw what had happened, they ran off and told it in the city and in the country. Then people came out to see what had happened, and when they came to Jesus, they found the man from whom the demons had gone sitting at the feet of Jesus, clothed and in his right mind. And they were afraid. Those who had seen it told them how the one who had been possessed by demons had been healed. Then all the people of the surrounding country of the Gerasenes asked Jesus to leave them; for they were seized with great fear. So he got into the boat and returned. The man from*

whom the demons had gone begged that he might be with him; but Jesus sent him away, saying, "Return to your home, and declare how much God has done for you." So he went away, proclaiming throughout the city how much Jesus had done for him.

As is so often the case, to understand what's happening in this passage we need to begin by looking at what preceded it. This story immediately follows Jesus' calming of a storm that threatened to swamp the boat in which he and his disciples were crossing the Sea of Galilee. The disciples had been terrified, but when Jesus stilled the gale, they had a whole new reason to be terrified and asked, "*Who then is this*, that he commands even the winds and the water, and they obey him?" Jesus has left his home territory for the country of the foreign, pagan Gerasenes, which is tellingly described as "opposite Galilee." Between the two coasts is a liminal space of chaos and threat, where Jesus reveals his power over the forces of nature. In this act, Jesus asserts his own identity before confronting the demoniac whose self has been shattered.

The narrator's description shows us a man pushed beyond the boundaries of civilization, lost to the community, socially dead. In fact, he dwells among the dead, naked and tormented, uncontrollably violent and driven by his demons "into the wilds." He's the kind of person who is so far gone that others have lost sight of his humanity; they'd prefer to avoid him altogether, but if they can't, at least they can hope to control him. So thoroughly had this man been dehumanized that when Jesus asks him his name he responds with the name of his demons: "Legion; for we are many."[41] He has become completely identified with his condition; it's as if you asked someone their name and they replied, "Psychosis," "Unemployment," "Bitterness," "Regret."

Yet although the man is confused about his own identity, someone in there somewhere knows exactly who Jesus is: "Son of the Most High God." It's more than Jesus' own disciples have figured out at that point. Whether this is remarkable or not depends on who you think is speaking here. If it is the man himself, it shows a surprising level of insight. If he is literally possessed by unclean spirits, then you'd expect such to recognize their own enemy: "The devils also believe, and tremble."[42] Regardless, the narrator once again and even more explicitly pits Jesus' identity against the identity assumed by the possessed man, the holy against the unholy.

After a strange set of negotiations, the man is healed. We see a tortured soul restored: "clothed and in his right mind." In reality, he is more than restored, because we find him "sitting at the feet of Jesus," that is, in the position of a disciple. Now he does his own negotiating with Jesus: might he go with him, be with him, as one of his followers? Jesus (gently, I imagine) tells him no, he must stay where he is and tell his story. And here is another interesting detail that is often missed but is quite revealing: Jesus tells him, "return to your home, and declare how much *God* has done for you." And so the man proclaims through the whole city "how much *Jesus* had done for him." If he didn't know who Jesus was before, he knows it now and is not going to shut up about it even to people who only wanted Jesus gone so they could forget the whole upsetting episode.

There is one final point to notice about this story. As Karen Haig has noted,[43] the gospels record no other acts of Jesus in "the country of the Gerasenes." He makes a difficult crossing from Galilee, heals the demoniac, and returns to Galilee where he carries out further healings. In other words, Jesus seeks out this one troubled foreign soul, who had probably never heard of him and was likely beyond asking help of anyone, least of all some Jewish preacher from the "opposite side." The reason this story is so important is that it shows the lengths to which Jesus was prepared to go in order to restore one "spoiled" identity, to make whole one self that had been fractured into a "legion" of pieces. If Jesus would cross dangerous waters, destroy a lot of valuable property, and be run out of town just to heal one mad Gentile's identity, do you think he's not interested in yours?

Why We Need to Be Free

When I was a first-year graduate student, I took statistics from a gifted and famous scholar whom I looked on as something of a guide to the sacred mysteries. He would show up for class in his ancient corduroy trousers and shapeless sweaters and had a shock of untidy white hair reminiscent of either Einstein or a *Far Side* cartoon, depending on how I felt about statistics that day. Then he'd cover the board with equations that might as well have been magic spells for all I could follow them. At the end, he'd look over his shoulder, chalk still in hand, and say, "So it should be intuitively obvious, then, that . . ." I always felt that Professor Blalock's intuition, and likely that of everyone else in the room, was a good deal more advanced than mine.[44]

Likewise, Jesus: "Whoever has ears to hear, let them hear."[45] It often seems that the things Jesus says in the gospels either make complete, intuitive sense, or they make no sense at all, as if I have no ears. When Jesus says, "You will know the truth, and the truth will make you free,"[46] some people think, "Well right, of course," and read on. Others of us, perhaps those for whom overthinking everything is an occupational hazard, wonder: "Truth about what, and why would truth make us free?"

I'm actually working up to a confession here: In spite of all that I've just said about the importance placed in the Scriptures on God's identity and ours, I'm still not fully convinced. In that strand of Christianity that places a heavy emphasis on the experience of personal conversion, the decision to entrust oneself to Christ is the central life event. Once it's happened, then the main thing is to work on replicating that event in the lives of others. Clearly, people are expected to grow in the faith, but a lot of digging around in one's own psyche might be seen as a distraction from the work of evangelism.

God's priority list, then, would look something like this: He's very interested in saving us from the fires of hell, from dependence on our own righteousness for that salvation, and from the demands of the (Mosaic) law. He's also quite interested in saving us from our day-to-day screw-ups: the world, the flesh, and the devil. But in this particular corner of the church, you don't often hear about how God wants to save us from our false self, as such: from our illusions of self-importance; our chronic disappointment in ourselves; and our feeble bids for security, prestige, and control. Sometimes it seems that all these details will be taken care of the moment we breathe our last, so God's not going to invest a lot of time and energy in them now when there's other work (meaning evangelism) to be done.

This is not the neighborhood of the church where I've found a permanent home, but I've visited it and learned a lot there. The stress on personal conversion is a positive corrective to the "pray, pay, and obey" approach, where if you just do as you're told by the authorities, you're "in." It's the job of each of us to make the "faith of our fathers" (and, more likely, our mothers) our own; the call to personal holiness is universal. But none of this is incompatible with an understanding of conversion as a lifelong process, in which we keep turning over parts of ourselves until they are all healed and restored by God. It's just that if you've been influenced at all by the notion that God wants to save your butt from the flames and most of the rest is on hold until the afterlife (as I was, early on), then it may take a bit of extra work to believe that how you see yourself is really important in God's eyes. So I'd like to stay with this question a bit longer, and wrestle with it till my "intuition" kicks in.

In the Sermon on the Mount, Jesus described the values of God's kingdom: good deeds should be done in private; the treasure that matters is stored in heaven; and enemies are to be prayed for, not destroyed. He urged his listeners to seek this kingdom, to make it their whole life's goal, and assured them that if they did this, all other desires would be satisfied.

The thing is, you can only do this from a true self. The false self is too busy seeking its own needs—survival and security, affection and esteem, power and control[47]—to seek the kingdom of God. Let's return to Jesus' temptations in the wilderness.[48] Notice how each of them takes aim at one of the impulses of the false self:[49] "Command these stones to become loaves of bread." *You're safe, Jesus. You will always be able to meet your own needs, no matter what. Life need never be threatening for you.* "Throw yourself down." *The angels will be commanded to catch you, and everyone will know exactly who you are. They'll kiss the ground at your feet.* Finally, the kingdoms of the world are offered, for a price: "Fall down and worship me." *All worldly power is yours for the taking, Jesus. Just one small lie. Just once.*

So when Jesus told the people to seek God's kingdom first, he knew what the alternatives were, and just how seductive they could be. But he also knew that these things must be resisted, because if we allow them to, they will enslave us: "Everyone who commits sin is a slave to sin. . . . [But] if the Son makes you free, you will be free indeed."[50] Jesus' purpose in coming was to offer us this freedom, but like Ebenezer Scrooge, we often can't see our own chains. What would they look like if we could?

Sometimes it's easier to see someone else's chains than our own, and then work our way back. Our natural tendency to be judgmental can give us particularly keen vision for the speck in someone else's eye. This may not be such a bad thing if we immediately forget about it and consider what it might teach us about the log in our own. I was at a party recently where a number of the guests were fellow academics. A dispute arose between two of the men, whom I'll call Gary and Mike. The issue was one that is an important question in Gary's field, one on which Gary himself has done some of the key research. But Mike, who's in a completely different discipline, kept insisting on a point Gary knew to be wrong. As the debate wore on and the other guests grew increasingly uncomfortable, Gary kept suggesting they drop the matter: "This isn't the time; we can talk about it later." But Mike became more and more belligerent, insisting that he had a better grasp of the matter than the expert in front of him.

Why was this such a painful exchange for the rest of us to watch? I think it's because we were being treated to a very naked display of insecurity: Mike had his pants around his ankles but didn't have the insight to realize that his fragility was fully exposed. His false self was making an aggressive bid for recognition, prestige, and esteem. He was, in Goffman's terms, putting on an identity performance that was meant to convince the audience that he's a bona fide intellectual. His problem was that whenever people overperform a role, the audience stops suspending disbelief. All that's left is lights and greasepaint, and everyone gets up and goes home.

The false self is a cruel master. Mike was not free to simply enjoy a pleasant gathering of colleagues and friends, because his ego needs drove him to attack one of them. Do that enough times, and those colleagues and friends start finding a reason to be elsewhere. I don't know whether Mike came away from that encounter with what he was looking for. I only know that I felt sorry for him, and I'm pretty sure that's not what he was looking for.

So what does this little meditation on the speck in my brother's eye teach me about the log in my own? Macho, aggressive displays of expertise, in which one person wins by talking over the opposition, are not really my style. I don't have enough testosterone, and in any case, I gave up on being an expert years ago. My problem is more stereotypically feminine: I'm a people pleaser, and this causes me to lie.

As I was growing up, I somehow acquired the belief that it was my duty to ensure that the people around me were comfortable and amused. Young girls of my generation, like those before us, were taught that if we couldn't be pretty and pleasant, cheerful and charming, we should make ourselves scarce until we were fit for human company. This is a very different role and requires a very different performance, which I kept up as well as I could as a young adult, through personal trauma and significant depression. I hate conflict and find it easier to subordinate my needs to those of others than to be direct about what I want.

Another story from graduate school: I had a close friend at that time who used to come to my apartment in the evenings. We'd watch movies, order pizza, drink wine, and talk about our courses, our dreams, and our cats until the small hours. On several occasions my friend said to me, "I know you would tell me if it was time to go home." She thought she could depend on me, as her close friend, to be that honest. But that would have violated the prime directive: be pleasant. So I, as a morning person, would stay up hours later than I wanted to and still be up before six the next day, because I would never tell a guest in my home that it was time to leave.

Being a people pleaser in a society of people pleasers would work pretty well, because everyone would defer to each other's needs. Everyone would assume that they needed to be courteous and play by the rules, because that's the only way people pleasers' needs get met, since they can't ask. That our society is not composed entirely of people pleasers should be "intuitively obvious," even if you're not a sociologist. The dark side of being a pleaser is that I have a zealous inner cop who monitors the infractions of others and wants to go around writing citations for them. All forms of inconsiderate behavior get my inner cop going: people who play their music too loud (that is, where I can hear it), who talk at full volume on planes when others are trying to sleep, and who leave their shopping cart in the center of the aisle are all lawless thugs who need to be punished.

I was baffled by the degree to which discourteous behavior upset me, until I realized it's because it taps into a deep fear that my needs won't be met. The false self that is preoccupied with survival and security meets the false self that needs affection and esteem, and the result is a resentful paralysis: there are things I want, but I'm too "nice" to ask for them. Instead, I lie and pretend everything's all right. Then I suck up my irritation as long as I can, building up a full-scale grievance. If it's an ongoing relationship, then the process is likely to end in either sudden explosion or sudden withdrawal: I'll either nuke the person bothering me or, more likely, just disappear with no explanation, never to be heard from again. This process is not pretty, pleasant, or amusing, and it does feel rather like a set of chains.

But God is merciful, and we don't have to be stuck in these patterns forever. Among the "fruits of the spirit," or changes we should see if we are deepening in faith, are things like patience, generosity, and peace.[51] I'm sure Jesus mentally adds "a sense of humor" to St. Paul's list every time he reads it. In the Jungian tradition, achieving personal integration requires recognizing and befriending our shadow side. The "pleaser" is really the shadow of my compassionate and generous self, so the "inner cop" is the shadow of a shadow. Now that I'm aware of this, I am learning to spot my inner cop, feed her a doughnut, and send her on break when she gets out of hand.[52] This probably helps keep my blood pressure down, but why should it be that important to God? Why is it this false self, in addition to death and damnation, whatever that might mean, from which the Son wants to make me "free indeed"? I think at least part of the answer is this: *As long as I am obsessed with other people's violations, I cannot see that they are shining like the sun.*

In other words, my false self is psychotic, out of touch with reality, and Jesus wants me "in my right mind" every bit as much as he wanted it for the Gerasene demoniac. He wants me to recognize his image in others, and I will be much more able to do this with eyes that look out from a true self, stripped of illusions both comforting and cruel. One of the things people most admire about Francis of Assisi is that he saw Christ in everyone, the greatest and the least, and this radically changed how he treated them. As he began to move away from worldly pursuits and turn his thoughts toward God, Francis one day encountered a leper[53] on the road. Having had a lifelong aversion to lepers, well beyond most people's at that time, Francis initially was content to toss the man a few coins and ride on. But a moment later something stopped him, and he rode back, dismounted, and embraced the outcast man, touched the untouchable.

Most of us can recognize this as the act of a holy man: to see the divine image where it is most hidden, and love one's neighbor when it is most challenging, even when that neighbor is a leper. But what if the leper is us? One way to read the story is that Francis's conversion involved embracing those parts of himself that he most loathed, growing up spiritually to the point where he could "love his neighbor *as himself*"—that is, with honesty and compassion. "For me," Thomas Merton said, "to become a saint means to be myself. Therefore the problem of sanctity and salvation is in fact the problem of finding out who I am and of discovering my true self."[54]

Being holy, being "Christlike," means having what St. Paul called "the mind of Christ,"[55] and there is no doubt about how Christ treated those whom everyone considered beyond the pale, including themselves. Can we do this, or at least aspire to it? If I have discovered my true self and seen my leprous flesh transfigured, then when I encounter another soul tortured by wounds without and within, my attitude will be different. I will believe in that person's worth, know that they are shining like the sun, not as an abstract concept but as a truth I have lived in the depths of my own soul. Does healing our broken sense of self matter to God? You will judge for yourself, but I think I am convinced.

Chapter 4

Made for Freedom: The True Self

Becoming more fully yourself is not a kind of license to be whatever you think you might want to be, but it is a deeply demanding search for honesty and penitence before the face of the Holy.

—Rowan Williams[1]

Have you ever noticed how medieval writers go on about virginity? Clare of Assisi, for example, in her first letter to Agnes of Prague, addresses her as "the esteemed and most holy virgin, the Lady Agnes."[2] Clare goes on to tell her that in rejecting the emperor and consecrating herself to Christ, she has chosen a far better bridegroom:

> You took a spouse of a more noble lineage, Who will keep Your virginity ever unspotted and unsullied, the Lord Jesus Christ:
>
> When You have loved [Him], You shall be chaste; when You have touched [Him], You shall become pure; when You have accepted [Him], You shall be a virgin.[3]

Clare's words seem to suggest that Jesus is the best bridegroom because Agnes could give herself to him without losing herself in the process—that is while remaining, in some important sense, *intact*.

Holy women in those days were always running around consecrating their virginity to God, in a way that seems kind of neurotic to us now. One would've thought one's heart, soul, mind, and strength would be enough. The church of the Middle Ages seems obsessed with virginity, as if holiness of hymen were a cardinal virtue. Of course, there were reasons for this that were very *un*spiritual. A virgin bride typically brought a larger dowry to a marriage, garnering more generous gifts in return from the family of the groom, and virgins who entered religious life would bring that dowry to the church. In medieval Europe, a woman's identity and worth could be culturally reduced to her sexual role, whether she was married off to an earthly or a heavenly bridegroom. She was either a means of producing children a man could be reasonably sure were his own, or she would literally embody holiness, being safely tucked away where she could represent an ideal of quasi-angelic unfallenness. Regardless, church and society agreed that a woman's virginity was a measure of her value: "The main quarrel between religious and secular authorities was whether virginity was spendable earthly coinage or ethereal heavenly treasure."[4]

As foreign as this may seem to us now, and as much as I've always deplored the church's preoccupation with sexual "purity" over other kinds, such as purity of economic relations, of our treatment of each other, and of the earth, I think I see what they were getting at. I recognize a kind of virgin impulse in the innocent ardor of Clare's words, and it's an impulse I can relate to. This is not because I want to turn back my personal clock (as if I could). It's because I understand the desire to offer something to God that has never been given to anyone else, something that's never been compromised or sold out, never cheapened by thoughtlessly sharing it with someone less worthy, or sullied by putting it to base purposes. Thomas Merton recognized this impulse too, and called the place it comes from the *point vierge*.

The virgin point. The still point. The *point vierge* is the holy of holies within each of us, a place pure enough to house God himself. As Merton explains:

> At the center of our being is a point of nothingness which is untouched by sin and by illusion, a point of pure truth, a point or spark which belongs entirely to God, which is never at our disposal, from which God disposes of our lives, which is inaccessible to the fantasies of our mind or the brutalities of our own will. This little point of nothingness and of absolute poverty is the pure glory of God in us. It is so to speak His name written in us, as our poverty, as our indigence, as our dependence, as our sonship. It is like a pure diamond, blazing with the invisible light of heaven. It is in everybody, and if we could see it we would see these billion points of light coming together in the face and blaze of a sun that would make all the darkness and cruelty of life vanish completely. . . . I have no program for this seeing. It is only given. But the gate of heaven is everywhere.[5]

This is a point of "absolute poverty," because we have never been able to add anything to it. It remains entirely the creation of God, and that's just as well because whenever we add things that seem like a good idea to us, we usually end up having to clear them away later on. The *point vierge* is the image and glory of God within us, a place of perfection that anticipates our resurrected and glorified selves. Its purity remains *intact*, however messed up everything around it. This is why we should reverence the glory of God in every person, including the most despised and degraded, including even ourselves. Every human heart contains the throne room of God.

Beyond being the purest part of ourselves, the *point vierge* is the "gate of heaven," the place where we meet God. In the tradition of bridal mysticism, which emphasizes the soul's intimacy with God,[6] this is the nuptial chamber, where the two are able to shut out everyone and everything else and delight in their union. In *The Flowing Light of the Godhead*, the thirteenth-century German mystic Mechthild of Magdeburg parts the curtains and give us a glimpse inside:

> Then the bride of all delights goes to the Fairest of lovers in the secret chamber of the invisible Godhead. There she finds the bed and the abode of love prepared by God in a manner beyond what is human.
>
> Our Lord Speaks: "Stay, Lady Soul."[7]

The exchange that ensues is a beautiful picture of mutual surrender and freedom. Christ reassures the soul of her closeness to him, of the glorious destiny in which all her heart's desires will be fulfilled. He then invites her to cast off the awkward outer garments of fear and shame. This is essential, because as long as fear and shame occupy our attention, we are locked in the prison of ourselves.

A focused gaze on God requires inner freedom, the freedom to drop our morbid obsession with self and look beyond. When we lack this freedom, we're like a woman in a strapless dress who's not entirely confident it's going to stay up. Instead of relaxing and enjoying the occasion, she's constantly checking and adjusting it, and let's face it: a woman who spends the evening staring at her own breasts is just not that charming. We spend so much of our lives like that: "Oops, I just had an unkind thought, sorry Lord"; "Oh wow, that was an ugly, judgmental comment. Help me not to be like that"; or "There it is again, a surge of ego. When will I stop wondering what others are thinking of me?" We tug and tug at our dress, and no matter how beautiful it may be, all that fussing is bound to detract from its allure.

But at the *point vierge*, we are as unself-conscious as little kids at the beach. They're not worrying about their bodies, their bathing suits, and their tan lines; they just enjoy themselves in a freedom most of us can scarcely remember. In short, they are being their true selves. While the basic components of the false self are already in place, it has not yet become the fortress it will be by adulthood, which is why Jesus urged us to become like little children. Kids are self-centered, to be sure. But their capacity for delight can help them transcend that for a time, while they lose themselves in a tide pool.

Glimpses of the True Self

What if we could do that? What if we could be that free from preoccupation with our self? The examination of conscience is a necessary part of the spiritual life, so I'm not saying we should never look inward. On the contrary: there are plenty of people who could use a lot more of that. But for those of us who can't stop gawking at our inner train wreck, there comes a time to put self-scrutiny aside and look elsewhere. Here's a little thought experiment: Try to imagine yourself as a completely beautiful human being, inside and out. Begin by imagining yourself physically: anything and everything you'd like to change about your appearance would be just what you'd like it to be. Further, nothing about your body could ever embarrass or betray you: your hair could never be out of place, your teeth couldn't hold onto spinach, and nothing socially unacceptable would be emitted by your innards. Your breath is always sweet, your joints never ache, and you never look tired. Got that picture?

Now go in deeper: Imagine your inner self completely at ease. There is no need to protect, produce, or perform. You cannot look stupid, so you don't need to pretend you know things you don't. You don't have to make your motives look purer than they are. Everything about your personality, your life, your choices, is fully known and fully accepted, even cherished. You can ask any questions you want, without worrying about being seen as impertinent or intrusive. If the answer to any request is "No," or "Not yet," you know you will be able to accept it without taking it personally, confident that it's in your best interests. You have nothing to gain, nothing to lose, and nothing to prove. You just are, and who you are is just right.

True Selves Vary

Hold that image in your mind for a moment while we consider how different everyone's version would be. One of God's greatest gifts to us in creation is diversity; think of what the rich variability of terrain, of plant and animal life, and of humans tells us about the creative mind of God. God obviously rejoices in difference, whereas we humans often struggle with it. History is full of the tragic consequences of our inability to cope with differences of skin color, hair texture, and facial features, not to mention tribe, religion, and sexuality. There is tremendous pressure today to conform to culturally defined expectations of body size and shape. But we can also feel pressure to conform to certain personality types, especially when people who exemplify those types are seen as smart, successful, and otherwise desirable. When we're in close relationships with people whose personalities or temperaments are very different from our own, we quickly start doing what humans usually do: turning differences into rankings, variation into inferior and superior.

Consider the difference between introverts and extroverts. This difference is not so much about being shy versus outgoing, but about how we're affected by contact with people: extroverts gain energy from being around others, while introverts find social interaction draining. Although most introverts do enjoy being with others, they usually prefer the company of one or two close friends to the scene at a big party. Even after an evening with the people they love most, however, introverts need time alone to recover.

You can imagine how quickly an introvert married to an extrovert could come to be defined as socially inept; it doesn't take much more imagination to see the introvert viewing the extroverted partner as shallow. One of the most helpful tools I've found for getting past these negative comparisons is the Myers-Briggs Type Indicator (MBTI). The MBTI is an instrument developed in the 1940s based on Carl Jung's theory of personality types.[8] Combinations of four basic dichotomies (extroversion/introversion; sensing/intuition; thinking/feeling; and judging/perceiving) produce sixteen recurring personality types, each with distinctive ways of thinking, acting, and interacting.

I admit that when I first heard of the MBTI, I thought it sounded like a cross between astrology and those silly quizzes you find in certain women's magazines. When I checked with a couple of friends who are research psychologists, however, I learned that while the MBTI has been around a long time and isn't exactly cutting any psychological edges, it has got a solid foundation in a major personality theory and is considered a useful and accessible way of getting insight into oneself and others.

The most important insight I've gained from the MBTI is that people come as *packages*. That is, there are certain constellations of traits that tend to recur together, so that an individual whose traits make up a particular package will predictably be good at some things and less good at others, will place priority on some things and not on others. This is not to trivialize or stereotype human psychological differences but to help us make sense of them and of ourselves. The developers of the MBTI stress that the types are all equal; no type is "better" than any other, and none is "worse." Each is just a particular style, one package among many.

When I looked at my own type and considered how it affected my horizontal and vertical relationships, some things began to make sense. I am an INFP/J; that is, my types are introvert, intuitive, feeling, and midway between judging and perceiving. Among the characteristics of "intuitive types" is that they like to focus on the big picture and think about the meaning and potential in a situation. They're dreamers and visionaries, who work well with symbols, images, and metaphors. By the same token, they're not good at mastering or remembering facts and tend to let the details slide. They're also terrible at giving directions.[9]

This explains a lot, like why I can watch a football game carefully and understand what's happening at the time, but once a given play is over I don't remember what happened. I will remember who won, at least until the next day. Understand that we are season ticket holders and I've gone to virtually every home game my university has played since the early 1990s. I dread being asked for directions, as I often have no idea how I get places and have been known to get lost going home from work. This also helps me understand why I always lose a certain kind of argument with my husband. Although he is a deep thinker and has worked with the "big ideas" in his field, he is also the consummate fact man. It's not that he thinks he's always right; he usually *is* right. He not only has the whole game stored in his memory as we leave the stadium; it'll still be there the next week, the next month, the next season. He also remembers exactly how many times I promised to pick up the dry cleaning and didn't do it and how many times we took the vacations I wanted and not the ones he would have chosen.

I have learned that I never win these arguments, so the sooner I change the subject, the better. What's really important, though, is that I've learned that my mind is not inferior just because it doesn't work the way his does. It's just different, and also has certain strengths that predictably go with my "package" and not with his. I'm sensitive to the motivations behind people's actions. I love to play with words and images, and I'm good at learning languages. But if you want someone who's going to remember details, you shouldn't look to me any more than you'd choose a golden retriever as a guard dog. My mind doesn't work that way, but that's not the same as saying "my mind doesn't work." A golden retriever is just right as a loving, fun family dog, and I am just right for some things too. This is who I really am, and thinking about it this way helps me accept this self.

The MBTI has also helped me understand some things about my spiritual self. Here's a description of the INFP at prayer:

> INFPs usually dislike set forms of prayer and prefer a more personal, spontaneous response to God. INFPs like to look at

> prayer not as a formal duty but rather as a time of joyful communion. . . . They need to take time just to sit and be still and wait for the Lord to make known His will to them. This will result in experiences of a deep union of love with God and with the whole world.[10]

Reading this has helped me understand why, after many years of trying, I still find it difficult to make a regular practice of saying the Daily Office, the services of morning and evening prayer required of Third Order Franciscans in my province. Although I love liturgical worship in a group setting, when I am alone it just gets in the way. It'd be like going to dinner with my husband and having to recite the first two acts of *Hamlet* before we can talk to each other. Since in the edition I have before me those two acts run to about fifty pages, dinner would likely be over before we got to have any real conversation. Likewise, if I spend the time I have set aside for prayer on the Daily Office, that time will run out before I get to pray the way I feel called to, the way that really sustains me and deepens my relationship with God.

For me, the Daily Office doesn't feel like prayer; it feels like an obstacle to prayer. And yet, there are many people for whom the Office forms the basis of a rich and satisfying prayer life. Different personality packages will likely predispose us to different types of prayer, so that the particular ways people find to "gaze" at God will also differ (and we'll look at those differences more closely in chapters 7 and 8). As with the Myers-Briggs types themselves, however, one of these spiritual "styles" is no better or worse than another. I could see myself as a "failure" at the Daily Office, or I could appreciate the fact that prayer for me is "a deep union of love with God and with the whole world." I may be a little undisciplined, but on the other hand, I sometimes see people shining like the sun.

"Celebrate diversity" has become such a cliché, but I really wish we could celebrate our spiritual differences instead of using them to diminish others or ourselves. Our rich diversity is the image of an infinite God within us, and we should treasure it. On a practical level, the MBTI, like the Enneagram and similar instruments, can help us move toward understanding and accepting, even treasuring, our true self. Along with the contemplative gaze, these tools can be used by God to heal the wounds within us, and that healing will affect our relationships with God, with others, and with ourselves.

Praying from the True Self

Now, back to the person you envisioned as your perfected self. If you approached others as this person, this whole, unbroken self, how do you think it would change the ways you deal with them? Let's look up first and then out. If you came before God as this self, how would your relationship to God change? It might be helpful to think about some of the different forms of prayer and imagine how each of them might evolve.

Confession would likely be one of the more striking areas of change. To come to God as a self that is not perfect, but is whole and true, would mean neither denying nor exaggerating our faults. We'd see them clearly and regret them sincerely, but we would not hide in shame and avoid showing up at all. Nor would we try to cover up, pass the buck, or otherwise deny our own culpability. These techniques didn't work for Adam and Eve, and they don't really work for us either. Of course, when hiding and denial fail and we realize the game is up, we often change course, cringing and beating our breasts, declaring ourselves the chief of sinners. We throw ourselves at the feet of the angry judge, who's been waiting for us to slip up so he can send us to hell. So whatever sin we showed up with, we have now added idolatry, having prostrated ourselves before a god of our own imagining.

It's not hard to see how this happens. Think of our reaction when a public figure is involved in a scandal. Especially if it's a religious leader who's been a heavy-handed moralizer, and he gets caught with his pants down. Or a politician of the other side, who's discovered with her hand in the till and is publicly humiliated. On our better days, we might feel a bit of charity, even utter a prayer for them. On our lesser days, our lesser selves enjoy seeing people get taken down a notch, and the more we think they deserve it, the sweeter their fall.

The mistake here lies, again, in creating God in our image, projecting the emotions of the false self onto God. But God is not like our false self. God is love, and love "does not rejoice in wrongdoing, but rejoices in the truth."[11] When you love someone, like your child or your best friend, and they do something really despicable, you don't rub your hands together and say, "Ah, I always knew she'd come to no good." You feel anguish; you grieve the disconnect between the person you love and the thing they've done. You know it's going to hurt them, and it hurts you too. If we could just see what God sees—ourselves radiant, transfigured, beloved—then it might be easier to believe that what God most desires in that moment of our penitence is to wrap us in his embrace. Then maybe instead of hiding, excusing, or berating ourselves, we could trust that God shares our sorrow but sees the big picture and understands the concept of a work in progress.

In petition, we come to God with our own needs, and in intercession, we come with the needs of others. How would these prayers change if we prayed them from our truest self? From what we know of the false self, we would expect that its requests would be driven by its principal needs: safety and security, affection and esteem, power and control: "Lord, I need a promotion/a spouse/a convincing argument that proves I'm right." "Please make sure that I never suffer, am never alone, never confused and disoriented, never doubt myself, or you." "Please ensure that nothing scary ever happens to me, or to people I love. And if you don't, I might take my business elsewhere."

I'm not saying we shouldn't bring human need before God—our own and others'. Jesus himself taught us to pray for our daily bread. But he also taught us to pray "thy will be done," and modeled that prayer for us when it was hardest, and cost him bloody sweat. Yet what a difference it makes to pray "thy will be done" when you know God delights in you, and has paid such a price for the sole purpose of drawing you close so that you can, in the words of the Westminster Catechism, "enjoy him forever."[12] When you can go beyond parroting the words and truly believe in the depths of your heart that God created you for joy, then it's easier to accept that the path to joy may lead through places that are not so enjoyable in themselves. Once you fully trust that God has called you "Beloved," then when things go dark around you, you can resist the temptation to suspect it's because God doesn't really care. And when your need is the greatest, you won't have to start out with a lengthy preamble about how little you deserve God's help. You'll have the freedom to climb into the lap of a tender and devoted Mother and know that, whatever the outcome, your well-being is her deep desire.

Our prayers of adoration and oblation (the offering of oneself to God) would be radically transformed if we prayed them from a true self. Perhaps these prayers are really only possible from a true self; at least, they are likely to well up from the truest part of ourselves. The Catholic doctrine of purgatory suggests that a lot of the grime we've accumulated will need to be scrubbed away before we're ready for the Beatific Vision—the resurrection experience of adoration in which we meet God face-to-face. And in spite of disagreement about the process, how it works and what to call it, Protestants too know that the majority of us will not take the current version of ourselves straight into the divine Presence. Whether you think the process is a long one or instantaneous, whether you think it requires suffering or is basically a glorified spa treatment, we all know that God is not going to make us spend eternity as the broken, unfinished creatures we are now. The false self is going to have to be finished off, or our joy would never be complete.

But remember: *that transformed version of you is known and present to God right now*. God dwells in eternity, and is already intimately acquainted with this version of you. If you can trust this, then you can reach out and allow God to help you step through the veil between time and eternity. On the other side, in the hidden place where he waits for you, you can be your truest self. That is the self that can be naked and unashamed, that can look, unflinching, straight into the face of God. And when we look into that face and know ourselves beloved, it will be the most natural thing in the world to lay all that we have and all that we are at his feet.

The True Self Is Known by Name

I've suggested that true freedom and joy come from learning to trust that God has called you "Beloved." Before we consider how our relationships with others would change if we lived fully from a true self, let's consider how you might come to know that self as beloved of God.

Have you ever asked God what it's like being worshiped? When I did, I thought of my beloved dog Abby, now gone to rest. Abby's devotion was a thing as close to worship as I'll ever receive. How did it make me feel? When she looked at me with those adoring brown eyes, it didn't make me feel like an extraordinary person. It made me feel that she was a great dog, with a big, loving heart. Her adoration said nothing to me about the kind of person I was; it really spoke volumes about who she was, and the depth of the bond between us.

This is why I get a little frustrated when people say, "What kind of a God demands our worship? What sort of supreme being needs that kind of support for his ego?" When Abby gave me her love and trust, it wasn't about my ego. You'd have to be crazy to decide you were a good person because you're loved by a dog—especially a golden retriever, since they love everyone. Her love said that she was being everything a great dog can be.

Just so, God doesn't need my love or worship, but when I give them, it says to both of us that we are right where we should be, in right relationship. It says we have "the one thing that is needful," the very thing that life is *for*. And it's not going to be taken away.[13]

"I have called you by name," says the Lord, "you are mine." These words are spoken to Israel in the book of Isaiah,[14] and a few chapters later, God assures his people that he will never forget them: "See," he says, "I have inscribed you on the palms of my hands."[15] We have seen that in ancient Israel, the importance of a name went way beyond distinguishing between one person and the next. It was a way of summarizing who that person was, what their life was about. Throughout the Bible, people are renamed at critical junctures: Abram ("exalted ancestor") becomes Abraham ("ancestor of a multitude"); Jacob ("he supplants") becomes Israel ("the one who strives with God"); and Simon ("he has heard") becomes Peter (a "rock"). In each case it's as if God is unearthing the true self hidden beneath layers of accretion and giving that self a name that speaks the truth about it to the person being named and to the world.

But this treatment is not just for biblical celebrities. As we learn in the Revelation to St. John on Patmos, God longs to confer on each of us our true name. The church at Pergamum has messed up in numerous ways, but at least they have held onto their faith and have not denied Christ's name. To all those who hang on, he promises "a white stone, and on the white stone is written a new name that no one knows except the one who receives it."[16] So in one sense, the new name is a mystery. In another, I think, it isn't.

At his baptism in the Jordan River, Jesus was named by the Father: "You are my Son, the Beloved; with you I am well pleased."[17] "Well, of course, Jesus was the Father's Beloved," you're thinking; "what does that have to do with me?" Listen to Jesus at prayer:

> The glory that you have given me I have given them, so that they may be one, as we are one. I in them and you in me, that they may become completely one, so that the world may know that you have sent me and *have loved them even as you have loved me.*[18]

You could almost see "Beloved" as a family name, which we all share with Christ, and the name on the white stone as the one that is private, personal, like a first name that belongs to each of us alone. If so, we can start with the assumption of our belovedness and then seek out the name God has for our own self in particular. How would we go about that?

When we are seeking the things of God, it's generally a good idea to begin by asking for help. In a talk titled "Staying Spiritually Healthy," Rowan Williams put it this way:

> [S]ustaining "life in the spirit" under pressure, I think, has rather a lot to do with retaining the ability to say to God, "Tell me who I am." Because I'm not going to settle with what everybody else is telling me—I'm not even going to settle with what I'm telling me. I'd like to hear from you. . . . I'd like to hear you saying my name.[19]

Of course, if you're going to ask God to speak your name, it'll help if you'll get quiet enough to hear it. Busyness and distraction are death to this kind of prayer; it needs focus and attention. Archbishop Williams goes on to say that "the real problem in prayer, the real difficulties arise, not with the absence of God but with the absence of me. It's not that God isn't there; it's nine times out of ten that I'm not."[20]

But Williams also raises another issue, that is, the difference between the names others give us, those we devise for ourselves, and the name God has for us. Sociology tells us that our sense of identity tends to be bound up in the roles we play and the groups with which we affiliate: our memberships in racial, class, nationality, political, religious, and other groups powerfully shape who we are and whether others are to be considered as "us" or "them." In fact, early experiments in social psychology showed that even groups devised in the lab, completely at random and without any meaning or content, quickly became the basis for in-group solidarity and intergroup hostility and competition.[21] But I doubt very much that the name on my white stone is "Middle Class, White American Sociologist," followed by my political and denominational affiliations, job history, and hobbies. That's not a name; it's a résumé.

If you want to know your true name, ask. Listen. Let God speak to you of your gifts and remind you where your passions lie. What are the values you most cherish? Who are the people you most admire—real or fictional?[22] Which of the saints, or which biblical characters, do you most identify with? Is there a single word or a short phrase that seems to sum you up? Does it make you feel free? When Jesus was called "Beloved" at his baptism, it's as if something was unlocked within him. After thirty years of quiet obscurity, suddenly things began to move. One of the things about Jesus that comes across powerfully in the gospels is his absolute freedom to be his own man in the face of all kinds of expectations from others. He had been called "Beloved," and when he faced the crowds, the king, the Roman governor, the unbelief of his own family, and the cluelessness of his friends, he made his own choices. I just don't see him getting through Gethsemane and going to the cross if he hadn't been sure of who he was and what he was doing. But he had been called "Beloved," and as often as he could, he sought out the One who had spoken that name. What else could have sustained him through such a hard life and agonizing death?

Whatever God's names for us, they all boil down to "Beloved." They convey something of God's delight in us, and they remind us that the gazing goes both ways. Allow me to quote Rowan Williams again:

> "All right, I've opened, I've calmed down, here I am . . . now what?" The answer God gives to that is, "Just stay there. . . .

> Sit still, because I like looking at you. I like the sight of you" says God. "It's not just about you contemplating me, in prayer" says God, "it's me contemplating you. . . . The real you, not the you that is hiding behind your memories and your fantasies and your hopes. Not the you that is half buried by this enormous furry grudge you're hugging to yourself, but *you*. The you I made, the you I redeemed, the you I love forever and ever. Just sit there and let me enjoy myself" says God.[23]

Secure in our belovedness, knowing ourselves to be an object of God's delight, we can move a step closer to the freedom Jesus had and that he wants us to share. How will that affect our relationships with the people around us?

Relating to Others from the True Self

"Everyone who commits sin is a slave to sin," Jesus said. "[But] if the Son makes you free, you will be free indeed."[24] If the false self is a slave to the ego needs of security, prestige, and power, then freedom is the hallmark of the true self. Freedom, as I've said, begins with knowing who you really are,[25] because you can't act freely from a self you've taken on like a part in a play, which has to be performed within the limits of the role. Once we've seen and begun to believe in that transfigured self, the self that God calls "Beloved," then freedom is the ability to live faithful to that vision, even if others disapprove. I am free in my relationships with others when I can say, as Jesus did, "I know this is not what you expected or wanted. Nevertheless, this is who I am, and I am not going to pretend otherwise."

Of course, the disapproval we have to make peace with may be our own. Here's a very concrete example of the kind of freedom I mean. Years ago, I made the decision to forgo the quest for tenure at my university and take a job as a senior lecturer. This means a lower salary, less security, and less prestige. I wanted to make room in my life for gazing, and for writing about what I'd seen, and I knew I could not pursue those things and the kind of productivity achieving tenure requires. There's no telling whether I'd have gotten tenure if I'd tried; plenty of people don't. But I made the decision not to try.

That was the easy part; the hard part was learning to live with that decision. Being a senior lecturer means being a second-class citizen in the academy, and every day that I go in to work, I know that I am not seen as a success. My colleagues, to the degree that they think of me at all (mostly we don't think of each other much), probably see me as a mediocre sociologist who does well enough in the classroom but is not playing in the big leagues. I'm not publishing much these days, don't attend conferences, and don't serve on important committees. In a world where having a national (better yet, international) reputation is everything, I am utterly obscure.

This is not necessarily the most comfortable way to spend one's career, and frankly, I've struggled to make peace with it. There is a stark difference between the way my false self and my true self deal with this situation, and this difference illustrates the freedom I'm trying to describe. My false self goes to work with a chip on her shoulder, thinking about being second rate and nursing the wounds to her ego. She's missing the esteem that would have come from being a successful academic and turns a critical eye on colleagues whom she sees as "playing the game"—too much in their heads, too involved in their own pursuit of prestige. In short, she despises others for being successful at the very thing for which she despises herself for failing at.

My true self, however, is surrounded by smart, decent people who have treated her well and respected her choice to pursue a nontraditional career. My true self looks inward and sees someone capable of making a bold move, of deciding what matters to her and finding creative ways to focus on it, and someone who can live with misunderstanding, even disapproval, if necessary. Jesus frequently disappointed the people around him, even those who cared most about him, because he knew who he was and what he was about. On my better days, when I'm leading from my true self, I know this security and freedom too. But I would not know it if I hadn't made regular visits to the place where Christ reveals to me who I really am. I do value excellence, and if I thought I were really just a mediocre, middle-aged academic, I don't think I could stay the course. But I've found, as Thomas Merton did, that "[i]n order to become myself I must cease to be what I always thought I wanted to be, and in order to find myself, I must go out of myself, and in order to live I must die."[26] Just as Jesus said.

Another way of thinking about this is that we know freedom in our relationships with others to the degree that we approach them without baggage. It's our emotional baggage, after all, that often triggers the ego needs of the false self. If you have a spouse who's been overly critical throughout your relationship (perhaps because she was the child of an alcoholic and grew up in a chaotic household so has a deep need for control), then even a truly innocent observation can be perceived as a reproach and put you into full combat mode. You overreact to your spouse's comment, because a perceived criticism is a threat to your esteem, which makes you feel insecure. Your overreaction is likely regarded as unfair; after all, it was just an isolated, harmless remark. Before you know it, the two of you are locked in the same old arguments, working from the same tired scripts that you both know by heart. Worse, you know the scene will end without any real resolution. And it all began with an innocuous comment. It was just one isolated incident, and you created all this drama out of it, because you have baggage.

The problem is that in a long-term relationship, there are no isolated incidents; everything comes with a history attached, and that history powerfully shapes how things are interpreted. This is true of interactions at the collective as well as the individual level and accounts for a lot of white people's sense that people of color are oversensitive and overreact to "isolated incidents," rather than recognizing that these events are part of a larger pattern and are cumulative. The ability to see individual people and events in a larger social and historical context is known as the "sociological imagination." It's one of the themes I harp on in my courses, because individualistic Westerners are not very good at this.

But our histories do shape us; our baggage entraps us in scenes we'd rather not play, or might prefer to play differently. What if we could? The Corinthians were assured that "anyone united with the Messiah gets a fresh start, is created new. The old life is gone; a new life burgeons! Look at it! All this comes from the God who settled the relationship between us and him, and then called us to settle our relationships with each other."[27] Of course, it's impossible to approach even a complete stranger without emotional baggage; that would be tantamount to having no history, and it takes pathology (amnesia) to do that. But surely my true self would at least pack a little more lightly. What might that look like in practice?

I've admitted to being a people pleaser, and for pleasers, the false self tends to lead with the needs for safety/security and affection/esteem. Getting people's affection and esteem makes me feel safe and secure, and if I don't please people, I'm afraid I'll lose these. So I put a mask over my true feelings, needs, and desires and play the part the way I think the audience wants to see it. I think my true self would be free from these preoccupations and able to assert herself when necessary. She wouldn't crumble in the face of criticism or opposition and would see conflict as inevitable and potentially healthy rather than as evidence that the sky is falling. One of the more frustrating things for the partner of a pleaser is our propensity to respond to criticism by catastrophizing: "Oh, then I must be a complete failure, the worst wife in the world." The tendency to rush to the bottom means that unless they're prepared for a lot of emotional upheaval, our partners can never bring up anything negative either. As long as neither party feels it's safe to bring up things that create unpleasantness, it's pretty hard for a relationship to move forward.

Saint Paul models a better way for us. If Paul had ever been a people pleaser, he was over it by the time of his ministry. As he said to the Galatians, whom he was in the process of chewing out at the time: "[A]m I trying to please people? If I were still pleasing people, I would not be a servant of Christ."[28] In the letter to the Ephesians (which was written, if not by Paul himself, then at least in the Pauline tradition), we are told to "speak the truth in love." We can see this again and again in Paul's letters to wayward churches, how he doesn't hesitate to tell them hard truths they need to hear but then assures them of his affection. As angry as he is with the Galatians ("You foolish Galatians! Who has bewitched you?"[29]), he calls them his little children, for whom he is going through labor. He adds that he wishes he could be with them in person, so he could change his tone.[30]

Most of us don't master that balance of truth and love, though; we either avoid speaking the truth and pretend that love is all positive feelings, or use "love" as an excuse to say hurtful things. Elsewhere,[31] I have written about the virtue of "chastity" as going way beyond our sexual ethics and being a more general principle of not exploiting other people. I agree with Franciscan Paul Jakoboski[32] that it's probably more helpful to call this "right relationship" rather than "chastity," as the latter term does not help people think of something besides sex. In either case, though, the point is that a true self leads not with its own needs in its relationships with other people but with theirs. If others are here for God's purposes and not mine, and if I strive to avoid seeing others as means to my own ends, then there will be times when I'll have to be able to tell them things they don't want to hear. But equally, I will take no pleasure in their discomfort. Jesus was not afraid to tell people they'd die in their sins if they rejected him, but he also wept over Jerusalem, knowing it would reject him, and miss "the things that make for peace" (Luke 19:42).

I am not suggesting that contemplation alone can bring us to this kind of balance. At least, not if you start out as unbalanced as I've been. For me, the search for this healthy point has also involved counseling, spiritual direction, reading, studying my sociohistorical context, and listening to a whole lot of people who are better at it than I am. In spite of all that work, I still have a very long way to go. What I am saying is that this process has to include discovering a true sense of self, because without that, we will remain trapped in our fears. I can't imagine asserting the self I sometimes see as a total failure, and even if that version of me found a voice, she'd only use it to try to make everyone like her. I'd spend my life like a neurotic dog, chasing its tail until it wears a circular groove in the ground.

But I have seen myself transfigured, and heard my name, "Beloved." I have visited the *point vierge*, the hidden chamber, and have known original innocence and freedom. I have allowed Christ to lead me to the mirror of himself and seen myself reflected there: radiant, perfected, shining like the sun. I have allowed him to write my new name on a white stone, and I have seen it inscribed on the palms of his hands. He has placed his own wounds, not on my hands and feet, like St. Francis, but on my heart, and nothing, not even death, can separate me from this transforming love.

It took me a long time to bring this self to my encounters with God. It's taking even longer to bring it to my interactions with others. It doesn't happen through contemplation alone, but contemplation is a critical part of the process: "As the lover gazes on the beloved and comes to an acceptance of self in God, the self is transformed as an image of God. The bridge between self-acceptance and transformation is contemplation."[33] Both sociologically and theologically, we know that we will find ourselves in the mirror of others. Contemplation is the choice to look in a mirror that will tell us the truth.

Chapter 5

The Gaze: Seeing the Face of God

[Y]ou cannot see my face; for no one shall see me and live.

—Exodus 33:20

Blessed are the pure in heart, for they will see God.

—Matthew 5:8

You can't just wake up one morning and decide to look God in the face. The ancient taboo on seeing God, or even "seeing" God by means of images, told ancient Israel many things, chiefly that their God was not like the gods of the pagan world. Israel's God was not an idol who could be bought off, controlled, or even understood, but the Holy One whose very name could not be spoken. In the world of ancient Israel, as we have seen, names had power; to know the name of another was to meet that other with a measure of strength. God told Israel his name so that they could be in relationship. But in case they were tempted to presume on this relationship, the name God gave them was mysterious, unfathomable, holy. They were not to take that name in vain, and to see the One who bore it was to die.

There were exceptions, however. The prophet Isaiah saw a vision of God enthroned in glory with six-winged seraphs calling out, "Holy, holy, holy." Isaiah knew he was in trouble: "And I said, 'Woe is me! I am lost, for I am a man of unclean lips, and I live among a people of unclean lips; yet my eyes have seen the King, the Lord of hosts!'"[1] What happens next is very telling: One of the seraphs takes a live coal from the altar and touches it to Isaiah's mouth. The seraph declares, "Now that this has touched your lips, your guilt has departed and your sin is blotted out."[2] Through a process of purification, which we have to assume was somewhat painful, Isaiah is made fit to see God.

When Jesus delivers the Sermon on the Mount, he takes it a step further: "Blessed are the pure in heart, for they *will* see God."[3] To see God's face, to be in such intimate relationship with our very Source, is what we were made for. It's the deepest desire of our hearts, though for most people, most of the time, it's buried very deeply indeed. But once we awaken to this desire, it becomes a hunger and thirst that can only be filled by Righteousness itself.[4] You can hear it in St. Paul's famous meditation on love, and in its fulfillment when perfect love is realized: "Now I know only in part; then I will know fully, even as I have been fully known."[5]

Both Jesus and Paul are saying that the perfection of love is our destiny, the meaning and purpose of life. Nothing short of this can satisfy our longing, and anything else we put in its place, even good things ("we know in part, and we prophesy in part"[6]), will become idols that break our hearts. But both suggest that this goal is at the end of a process of purification, of becoming a spiritual grown-up, and putting away childish things.[7]

The Path of Purification

What is this process like? Here we need to turn to the mystics, since this is their turf. Mysticism can be defined in countless ways, but probably the most basic is the "unmediated experience of God," which is exactly what we're seeking. One of the oldest and most enduring descriptions of the mystic path is divided into the states of purgation, illumination, and union. If you have masochistic tendencies you'd like to indulge, spend some time online investigating the variations on this theme; these will tie your brain into satisfying knots.[8]

At its simplest, however, the classic threefold mystic path looks something like this: Purgation is the state of newcomers to the spiritual life, whose primary task is to loosen their grip on sinful tendencies and start living something that resembles a Christian life.[9] It's the beginning of the end for the false self. The purgative way is Christianity 101, where we learn to stay out of drunken bar fights and stop being snotty to our neighbors. Everyone's purgation is different, so one person may need to learn a measure of self-control while another must become less calculating and more relaxed. Failures and losses in work, health, or relationships are especially efficient ways of chipping away at our false self and its illusions of competence and control. I understand that impending death is the shortest and most effective course of all.

The purgative state is a sort of spiritual house cleaning, and the work gets done in two ways: sometimes we scrub hard at the accumulated filth, and sometimes a great wind just comes up and blows a lot of crap out the windows. These active and passive purifications prepare the soul for illumination, but the process can take time, and it's easy to get stuck. When I was young, one of my favorite ways of torturing my parents was rock climbing, and the mystic ascent is reminiscent of a hard climb. You hang there on the side of a cliff, standing on something the size of a dime pasted on a wall, unable to find hand- or toehold for the next move. You realize you can't stay there and die of old age a hundred feet off the ground, and retreat is impossible because climbing down is always scarier than climbing up. You stay in that spot until your arms and legs are shaking from fatigue, and it begins to look like your next move is going to be a long and dramatic fall.

But then you find yourself on the summit and have no idea how you got there. In the soul's ascent toward God, it's as if he lets you struggle long enough to convince you that you really cannot do it and then puts a hand under each armpit and lifts you to the next ledge. It's an act of pure grace, in which God seems to be saying, "Relax now, I'll take it from here." In the illuminative state, things that were hard become easy, and virtues that were elusive become second nature. But the main thing about this state is that God has moved to the center. Until then, while I've believed in God and tried to act in a manner consistent with that belief, it's still mostly about me: I want to be a good person, be safe from hell, or have some self-respect.

When illumination comes, these concerns recede into the distance, because the basic premise of the relationship changes. We're no longer worried about passing a tough exam or appeasing a righteous judge. We've fallen in love, and all our energy, interest, and attention are in orbit around the Beloved. It's not a question of keeping score anymore; God delights me, and I want to delight him. Like any love relationship, this one is going to have its ups and downs; there can be plenty of trials, and a good bit of ongoing purgation, in the illuminative state. But everything has changed, because the motive has changed. We're no longer driven by fear or a need to prop up the self. We're driven by love.

Illumination is a kind of courtship, and it may go on for some time before it's sealed in the unitive state, the spiritual marriage.[10] Consistent with the spousal imagery used by numerous mystics such as Mechthild of Magdeburg and Bernard of Clairvaux, God and the human soul become one. But this is a "differentiated unity";[11] that is, while two become one, their separate identities remain intact rather than blending together into something new. In practical terms, this means that the person who experiences union with God not only retains her own identity but *grows into it.* She is transfigured; the true self that only God could see is increasingly the whole story, and the false self is left behind like the skin of a snake that has moved on.

When love reaches this point, it has burned away all other desires;[12] the heart thus joined to God is pure enough to meet him face-to-face, as Jesus promised. In one of his famous sermons on the Song of Songs, Bernard of Clairvaux characterized the mystical ascent as three kisses, which correspond to the purgative, illuminative, and unitive ways. The new convert is focused on penitence and conversion of life; he kisses Christ's feet. The one progressing in the spiritual life is permitted to kiss Christ's hand. The kiss bestowed on the mouth is reserved for those who have advanced to a very great love, by means of a great desire; as the Song says, "Let him kiss me with the kisses of his mouth! For your love is better than wine."[13]

The Interior Castle: *Moving Inward*

The sixteenth-century Spanish mystic Teresa of Avila[14] drew up a more elaborate and richly nuanced account of the spiritual journey in her most famous book, *The Interior Castle*. Teresa wrote with both passion and charm, plus frequent repetition and occasional ramblings, since she seldom reviewed what she'd written previously; she just picked up her pen each day and carried on. The result is a work that is exciting and personal but easy to get lost in. She's also not above confessing from time to time that she really doesn't know how to explain it, and she hopes the reader will figure it out.[15]

It's worth sticking with it, though, because Teresa's description of the spiritual journey is so profound, so insightful, and yet so down-to-earth. She wrote for her sisters, not for scholars, and, like Jesus, drew her imagery from everyday life: caterpillars and butterflies, gardens and fortifications. Her language was common, earthy, "subliterate"[16]—the kind of writing that in English might replace "going to" with "gonna." Teresa, the first female Doctor of the Church, diagnoses a problem highly relevant to our purposes,[17] so bear with me for a moment while I sketch out the architecture of her castle.

Teresa's analysis is based on the image of a beautiful castle "made entirely out of a diamond or of very clear crystal, in which there are many rooms, just as in heaven there are many dwelling places."[18] The castle is a series of concentric circles built around the innermost room, the "chiefest mansion,"[19] where the King dwells. The pilgrim soul must travel inward through a series of six mansions (also translated as "dwelling places" or "rooms") to arrive at last at the seventh mansion, the place of permanent union with God.

The journey begins in the outer courts, which are inhabited by snakes and other nasty creatures as well as guards who have no interest in entering the castle itself. This is the place of worldly souls, but once converted, the soul penetrates to the first two mansions where the simplest forms of prayer are learned, and the person works on shedding the encumbrances of the world. People often work hard at this stage, yet it's not unusual to find the occasional lizard scurrying over their feet, as old habits resist their efforts to change.

By the third mansion, however, they've managed to put together a reasonably convincing Christian life. A person in this stage attends church regularly, says his prayers, makes his donations, and generally avoids creating a scandal. Dwellers of the third mansion have their act together. They've got a well-regulated religious life: they know what's expected of them, and they do it, conscientiously and with real devotion. They pretty much look the way a Christian is supposed to look.

And this is just the problem. Because a person at this stage seems to have arrived, it's easy to imagine that there's no place else to go.[20] Teresa emphasizes that complacency in the third mansion can lead to getting stuck there when there are still three to pass through before we arrive at our goal. It's not just complacency, though; people also fail to move forward because they genuinely aren't aware that there's anything more. Or they think that if there is anything more, it's reserved for those intimidating, inhuman people from whom we distance ourselves by calling them "saints." We'll return to the problem of the third-mansion trap in a moment; for now, let's travel, as C. S. Lewis might say, "Further in and higher up."[21]

The fourth mansion represents a critical transition: from prayer as something we do to prayer as something God does. That is, this is where we go from "saying our prayers" to *praying*, from prayer initiated by us to contemplation, or prayer having its source in God. This is the point when God begins, in Rowan Williams's words, to "make a nuisance of himself."[22] We compose ourselves to pray, and it doesn't go according to plan. Perhaps God is vividly and disturbingly present, or he may be distressingly absent; either way, we are no longer in control. That whole tidy, intelligible religious life we'd carefully constructed seems increasingly beside the point, and we begin to suspect there may be a lot more to it than we'd imagined.

What's really happening at this point is the shift from fulfilling a set of religious duties to developing a real relationship. Except that it's more than a shift; it's really a kind of crumbling of the bridge and hurtling into the abyss. The next two mansions are an eventful time of consolation and desolation—terrible trials and temptations on the one hand, and on the other a sweetness and delight that makes one eager to endure them all. This is God's idea of courtship; brace yourself.

In the sixth mansion the King betroths the soul to himself, and in the seventh the spiritual marriage takes place. Here things are calmer: any visions, voices, emotional highs, and other phenomena that may have taken place earlier settle down, and a deep and lasting union brings with it "the most profound knowledge."[23] Here Teresa famously unites the gifts of Mary and Martha, contemplation and action, arguing that the soul in permanent union with Christ will exhibit both:

> For if [the soul] is with Him very much, as is right, it should think little about itself. All its concern is taken up with how to please Him more and how or where it will show Him the love

> it bears Him. This is the reason for prayer, my daughters, the purpose of this spiritual marriage: the birth always of good works, good works.[24]

That the mystic ascent ends for Teresa in good works shows that all this effort to reach the place we were made for, to become the fully realized human beings we were created to be, is not for ourselves alone. It's not an exercise in narcissistic navel-gazing, but the means of being ignited with the flame that fuels all good works and makes them possible.

I think it's safe to say that the more detailed a person's account of the spiritual journey, the less generalizable it is. That is, the more specifics they include, the more likely it is that the specifics of another person's quest will be different. Teresa has marked out a well-trodden path, but it is not the only path. It tends to be taken by those whose spiritual "style" is highly affective or emotional and who are comfortable with vivid imagery; this style of prayer is referred to as "kataphatic" and is typically contrasted with the "apophatic" way, which avoids both images and emotional extremes in favor of silence, darkness, and "unknowing."[25]

Both of these paths are tried and proven ways to union. But they are a bit like sexual orientation: if you're strongly identified with one, then the other is going to feel all wrong, though there are those who pray both ways. Probably the more one advances in prayer, the more one's spiritual practice begins to integrate the nondominant form. The important point, for our purposes, is that there is a *process* one must go through before real intimacy with God is possible. A person who charges into the castle straight from the outer courts and bursts unceremoniously into the throne room is not likely to be a loyal subject. Teresa also shows us that to have one's act together and stay within the boundaries of conventional piety is not the goal of the spiritual life. When St. Paul said that he trained hard for the race so that he could win the prize, I don't think perfect Sunday attendance and keeping his nose clean was what he had in mind.

I suspect he was thinking along the same lines as the fourth-century desert hermit, Abba (Father) Joseph:[26]

> Abba Lot came to Abba Joseph and said: Father, according as I am able, I keep my little rule, and my little fast, my prayer, meditation and contemplative silence; and, according as I am able, I strive to cleanse my heart of thoughts: now what more should I do? The elder rose up in reply and stretched out his hands to heaven, and his fingers became like ten lamps of fire. He said: *Why not become fire?*[27]

Abba Lot has been living in the third mansion, dutifully keeping his little rule and striving to control his thoughts. But he's begun to wonder if there isn't something more, and he's gone to the right place to find out. Abba Joseph has learned that the little prayers and fasts are just kindling, and no one collects kindling for its own sake.

We were made for so much more. We humans, in thrall to the false self, make both too much and too little of ourselves. We have a deep need to be "special," which leads us down the path of petty self-aggrandizement and trying to prove ourselves through our accomplishments. Our sense of self comes to rest on external measures of success and failure, and we preen or cringe according to whichever we think predominates. But even as we play with the cheap toys offered us by our culture—career, appearance, financial security—we seriously underestimate our true worth. The desire to feel special is mainly a problem because we want to feel "more special than others," and we use the wrong metrics to gauge whether we've succeeded. It's a desire that originates in the false self.

But the need for personal significance is not unhealthy in itself; in fact, I would say that God planted it within us as a sign pointing us toward our true identity and our rightful place in his family. In *The Signature of Jesus*, Brennan Manning recalls the story of Don Quixote and his romantic idealizing of the barmaid Aldonza.[28] He sees her as the Lady Dulcinea: beautiful, virtuous, and noble. The comedy lies in the contrast between Don Quixote's delusions and the reality of Aldonza, the tough and common little peasant. But the joke's on us, because Quixote, Christ-like, sees the real Aldonza, Aldonza transfigured. Dulcinea is the identity she was meant for, and by believing in it so strongly, he helps her to assume that identity and become her true self.

There are days when I could really use a Don Quixote to tell me that I'm beautiful, virtuous, and noble. My husband tries, though he isn't quite quixotic enough to turn me into a Dulcinea. But I think Jesus is. And being in a relationship with him means spending a lot of time delighting in each other's presence. I praise him, of course. But he also praises me, because that's what people do when they love. And he insists on treating me as nothing less than the transfigured vision of me that he sees, even if no one else does, including and especially myself. That treatment, over a period of years, has been a powerful means of healing a very broken sense of self.

From Rules to Relationship

To be able to receive that kind of healing, we have got to get out of the third-mansion trap. We've got to get past the idea that the spiritual life is about following rules and fulfilling obligations. We need to take seriously the idea that this is supposed to be a *relationship*. What would change if we did?

One of the first things that would change, I think, is that we'd stop "saying our prayers." I don't mean that you should never say grace again, or, heaven forbid, that you should not recite the Lord's Prayer. But if this is supposed to be a relationship, surely at some point we should stop talking and start listening. In chapter 9, I will offer a few suggestions for how one might try to do that, but the techniques are not all that important; what's important is that prayer stops being something we tick off our to-do list and becomes a form of interaction in which we invest real time and attention.

At the same time, we need to guard against taking an "achiever" mentality into prayer, and the deeper we go in prayer, the truer this will be. Again, there comes a point (for Teresa, the fourth mansion) when prayer becomes less and less about what we do and more about what God does. Carl McColman describes it beautifully:

> [C]ontemplation itself can never be reduced to a mere procedure. Contemplative prayer is not so much about *mastering* silence or *achieving* a desired state of consciousness as it is a gentle, unforced opening-up of your mind and heart—a simple gesture of allowing yourself to sit in the uncreated presence of God. In other words, contemplation is not something you achieve; it is something you allow.[29]

What else would change if we moved from rule keeping to relationship? A basic requirement for any satisfying relationship is that I must believe that the other person is interested in me and values my companionship. Unrequited love makes for good drama, but is not so great in real life. There needs to be mutuality. I don't need the other to like everything about me; I don't like everything about myself, and there are things about me that any honest person would agree need to change. But any close relationship, whether parent-child, lovers, or friends, needs to be based on mutual affection and respect. Where these are absent, the party with less power is going to end up in a servile, degraded position. There is a time to prostrate ourselves before the Ruler of heaven and earth. But there's also a time to walk together in the garden in the cool of the day. That was God's original intention, and when our primordial parents were avoiding him out of shame, God called out to them: *Where are you?*[30]

You can't just wake up one morning and decide to look God in the face. God has to restore us before we can face him; otherwise, the result would be shame, not joy. And it doesn't help that so much religion is shame-based. As we've seen, however, there is a process that prepares a person for that level of intimacy with the Holy One. Trying to circumvent that process is a bit like being introduced to someone, shaking hands, and then jumping into bed. It's likely to create problems, because the emotional intimacy is not commensurate with the physical intimacy; your body is acting like you're very close to someone who, in reality, you know almost nothing about and have no real reason to trust.

Likewise, you can't just rush up to Jesus and plant a kiss on his mouth. It's a good idea to begin at his feet, and this is why Clare advised Agnes to gaze into the mirror of the cross. There is a time, I believe, to gaze into the mirror of the risen Christ. But the cross is the place to begin, because before we can enter into relationship with him, we must believe that he loves us. And I don't mean being able to sing "Jesus loves me, this I know" in Sunday school; I mean being convinced, at the deepest level of our being, that this transcendent God, this utterly holy and unfathomable Other, loved me personally enough to endure the greatest suffering possible. If I cannot believe this, then true relationship is not possible, and I might as well take my choice from among the distant and capricious pagan gods, who have to be appeased with sacrifices and may still annihilate me in the end.

To try to live an ordered religious life without attending to this fundamental relational aspect is to practice the Christian faith without Christ—at least, without the real Christ. Jesus warned us that many would come in his name, claim to be the Messiah, and lead people astray.[31] Certainly there have been plenty of people over the centuries who have done that. But false messiahs can also come in the form of distortions of Jesus himself, and lead us astray when we believe things about him that aren't true. For those who suffer from a battered sense of self, one of the most persuasive false messiahs is the one who doesn't love us, who certainly doesn't like us, and has no great desire to be in relationship with us. This is a complete repudiation of the passion and death of Christ, and it is a lie. When Clare points us to the mirror of the cross, she is saying: "There—

this is who he is; this is how he loves. What does that love tell you about yourself? What does it say about your worth?"

The Church's False Selves

It would be nice if the church mirrored this back to us more consistently, but the false self is a problem at both the personal and collective, institutional levels.[32] The church is an incredible gift, and I wish I could explain that to those who want to know why you can't just follow Jesus without the encumbrance of "organized religion." It is the body and bride of Christ, and to be part of it is the greatest privilege and joy.

All the same, it's impossible, now as much as ever, to avoid seeing that bride as a bit of a slut. As I write this, Msgr. William J. Lynn of the Archdiocese of Philadelphia has just become the first senior official in the Roman Catholic Church to be convicted of knowingly shielding priests under his authority who were sexually abusing children. As an aside, I must add that although the media attention has focused on the Roman Catholic Church's abuse scandals, to imagine the problem is confined to that denomination is naïve. What's different about the Church of Rome is that it's a different kind of institution: having a large and powerful hierarchy has enabled it to add a layer of cover-up to the abuse problem itself, which might be harder in a smaller organization. But abuse happens everywhere.

Lynn was apparently motivated by a desire "to protect the church's reputation and avoid lawsuits."[33] I think we can agree that when the prime directive becomes protecting the institution at the expense of the weak and vulnerable, we have utterly lost all sense of who we are and why we are here. So one collective version of the false self might be called "The Institution Is Everything." As C. S. Lewis pointed out,[34] whether structures matter more than individuals depends on your view of the afterlife. If you don't believe that people live forever, then they come and go; institutions are what count, because institutions are what will be here after we're all gone, and they'll go on shaping the lives of people in the future. But if people do live forever, then we'll be around long after all social structures have passed away. Jesus consistently behaved in a way that valued humans above institutions, and if the church is to realize its true identity, it will have to do so as well, whatever the cost.

Another form of the church's collective false self might be called "Neo-Pharisaism," or "The Rules Are Everything." Jesus spent so much time hammering away at the version of this that existed in his day that you'd think his followers would be able to spot it a mile off and give it a wide berth. But it remains alive and powerful, and one place you can go to see, or rather hear, it in action is on the radio. I've confessed elsewhere[35] that I have a morbid fascination with religious radio programming, some of which is edifying but most of it is a theological and pastoral train wreck. There is one program in particular in which callers ask about the minutiae of church regulations and have various authorities tell them how to keep their crayons inside the lines. It's not that their answers are wrong; they're probably accurate enough, given the show's set of theological and ecclesial assumptions. It's that, after listening to dozens if not hundreds of hours of this program, the cumulative impression I'm left with is that it's very important to get your tithe of mint, dill, and cumin exactly right, but we're not going to talk about the "weightier matters of the law: justice, mercy, and faith."[36]

My own neighborhood of the church is not particularly beset by legalism, but we have our own versions of the collective false self, one of which could be called "A Nice Place for Nice People." As a denomination, we spend a good deal of time stuck in the third mansions, where everything is beautifully ordered—Episcopalians value good liturgy, music, and architecture—but we don't often challenge people to become fire. Like other churches, we do a lot of good works: we shelter the homeless, feed the hungry, and provide mosquito nets for people who live in malaria zones. We are pretty good at being inclusive, and giving people space to ask questions. But our adult faith formation is often haphazard and driven more by convenience than conviction: "So-and-so's available to talk about the upcoming referendum/organic gardening/her trip to Albania. Let's book her for the twenty-fifth." The result, all too often, is that nice people have nice experiences with other nice people, but if we're ever going to become fire, we'll have to find the matches on our own.

Both the church and the individuals within it need to be purified if we're to see God or ourselves clearly, which we must do if we're to reflect the Divine to a world that is gazing at us. Purification is painful, because it requires a self-emptying, or *kenosis*, of all that's false and destructive, so that truth and healing can fill the space. It means entering into a profound poverty, in which we relinquish ownership of everything that made the false self attractive and compelling in the first place. If we have the courage to let go and simply face God naked and with open hands, our vision will get clearer, and we'll discover a great secret: that very poverty is the road to liberation.

Chapter 6

Self-Emptying: The Privilege of Poverty[1]

The whole Christian life is a life in which . . . the more we progress, the poorer we get so that the man who has progressed most, is totally poor—he has to depend directly on God. He's got nothing left in himself.

—Thomas Merton[2]

I've been haunted lately by the word *kenosis*, the Greek word that refers to emptiness or emptying. It's the basis of the expression used in the famous hymn to Christ's humility that appears in the letter to the Philippians:

> Let the same mind be in you that was in Christ Jesus,
> who, though he was in the form of God,
>   did not regard equality with God
>   as something to be exploited,
> but *emptied himself*,
>   taking the form of a slave,
>   being born in human likeness.
> And being found in human form,
>   he humbled himself
>   and became obedient to the point of death—
>   even death on a cross.[3]

The hymn goes on to say that God's response to this humility is to give Jesus the name above every name, at which every creature in heaven, on earth, and under the earth will ultimately bow, confessing him as Lord. On a smaller scale, this is how it works for the rest of us too: as Jesus himself said, "all who exalt themselves will be humbled, and those who humble themselves will be exalted."[4] So we are to have "the same mind" as Christ, and this involves humbling and emptying ourselves. *Kenosis.* How do we do that?

Mostly, I think, we don't. That is, most of us don't take the path of *kenosis* voluntarily. We don't really empty ourselves; we have to *be* emptied, and much of the time that happens through various forms of loss. We lose people who are dear to us. We lose a job, or a whole career, through downsizing, or failure, or scandal. We lose everything from our health to cherished ideas, even, sometimes, our idea of God.

And in every major form of loss, there is the potential for a corresponding loss of self. If I lose my spouse, I lose my identity as a married person and take on that of a widow or divorcée. I lose my health, and out goes my identity as a person who is active and self-sufficient. In my twenties, I lost my faith, and with it went my identity as a Christian. That was devastating, as it was the core of who I was and the meaning of my life. Major life transitions, like retirement or the empty nest, can create a deep sense of doubt within. It's as if the long-running show has finally closed, and we're left without a character, without a role: who am I supposed to be now? The fact that these two passages are totally predictable does not mean they can't take us by surprise, and shake us to the core. *Kenosis.*

I suspect that most of the people who will eventually lose themselves at retirement or when the nest empties actually lost themselves years ago, in the roles of "worker" or "parent." Much of the time this happens through processes that are basically benign, or at least well intended. The demands of life just keep us from pausing long enough and often enough to keep in touch with who we are, and little by little we're submerged in our roles until we become them. But sometimes the self is not lost so much as stolen. An abusive, belittling partner's constant derision can chip away at your self-worth. Likewise the partner who trades you in for a newer, more glamorous model can scoop out your identity and leave you hollow inside. *Kenosis*, indeed.

Even more calculating is the "gaslighter," the person who deliberately creates situations and interactions that cause you to doubt your sense of reality.[5] I had a roommate like this when I was eighteen and had just left home. She was one of four members of our household, a few years older and a great deal savvier than I. She'd taken a strong dislike to two of us and would react to things we'd say as if they were startling and disturbing. She'd move things around while we were gone and then pretend they'd always been that way, even subtly call our motives and ethics into question until we wondered about them ourselves. The two of us whom she targeted realized we were being manipulated by a master and moved out in time to keep our hold on reality. But it was a deeply unsettling experience, and there are those who don't bounce back so easily.

There are people who will try to shatter your mirror, and I know it's easier said than done, but don't let them. No one but God should have the last word on who you are. But no matter how stoutly we resist, life will find endlessly creative ways to mess with us, and when the upsets are significant, they can shake loose our sense of self until it feels like rubble. *Kenosis.* How is it a good thing when my self feels like water poured out into sand?

Poverty in the Franciscan Tradition

I think I can begin to grasp the positive side of *kenosis* when I see it as a form of poverty, which is one of the core values of my own Franciscan tradition. That in itself requires some explanation. Saints Francis and Clare both made poverty the heart of their spirituality. They didn't just think it was quite a nice idea; they were infatuated with it. In fact, Francis declared Lady Poverty his bride and wed himself to her with all the passion of the young and the senseless. Clare, as I have mentioned, fought to the end of her life for the right of her sisters to live without even communal property, because she regarded poverty as the pearl of great price, the surest way into the heart of God.

A commitment to poverty continues to be a hallmark of Franciscan spirituality, but before I can explore this, I need to explain that there are three main branches of the Franciscan family, and they don't all pursue poverty in the same way. Franciscans of the First Order (active sisters and brothers) and the Second Order (contemplative nuns) live without personal possessions, though property may be owned by the community. We Third Order Franciscans, who strive to live the Franciscan ideal "in the world," make a vow of simplicity: we may own property but are expected to be mindful of our patterns of consumption and attentive to their effects on the world. In this discussion, I will use the words "poverty" and "simplicity" interchangeably, not because they mean the same thing, but to underscore the point that they are each embraced by Franciscans as different means to the same end.

We can think about poverty in two ways, external and internal, and each can be assumed either voluntarily or involuntarily. It should be said at the outset that there is nothing desirable or inherently holy about involuntary poverty; it is an evil that Franciscans, like all Christians, are called to confront. But voluntary poverty in material things is a witness against a society even more obsessed with consumption in our day than it was when the Franciscan movement began. And that's saying something.

The church itself needs this witness, since throughout its history it's succumbed to the lure of wealth and the power and prestige that go with it. Perhaps the crassest examples today are preachers of the "prosperity gospel," who teach that God will shower material rewards on us if we'll just have enough faith and send in our donations. Considering these people preachers of the Gospel is like dressing a slug in a tutu and calling it a ballerina. The prosperity gospel is a conspicuous boil on the backside of Christ's body; you have to wonder what they make of the poverty of Christ himself, since they see prosperity as a mark of God's favor. But there are more subtle versions around. Mostly these are sins of omission, in which the faithful are not told that the way of the pilgrim covers a lot of hostile terrain. They're not told that no one gets exalted without being humbled. They're not warned about *kenosis*.

But external poverty is only the beginning; the preparation for seeing God face-to-face requires inner poverty, an emptying of self that is harder and darker. It's an essential part of the process of uncovering our true self, however; as Ilia Delio has said, "When I ask the question, 'who am I?' I begin a life of poverty because the answer is one of radical dependency. I am not the source of my own life, rather, I come from God and belong to God."[6] A beautiful description of inner poverty is in Thomas Kelly's classic work, *A Testament of Devotion*. In a section on simplicity, he has acknowledged the importance of external paring down but calls the reader to take the next step:

> I have in mind something deeper than the simplification of our external programs, our absurdly crowded calendars of appointments through which so many pantingly and frantically gasp. . . . [T]here is a deeper, an internal simplification of the whole of one's personality, stilled, tranquil, in childlike trust listening ever to Eternity's whisper, walking with a smile into the dark.
>
> This amazing simplification comes when we "center down," when life is lived with singleness of eye, from a holy Center where the breath and stillness of Eternity are heavy upon us and we are wholly yielded to Him.[7]

Those who know this kind of simplicity, Kelly says, are marked by radiant joy and live in the "Fellowship of the Transfigured Face."[8]

This "centering down," this "singleness of eye," is really a question of focus. The reason people are still following Francis and Clare eight hundred years later is not because they embraced material poverty, important as that was to them both. The poor have always been with us, as Jesus promised. But if the point were just to run around in rags and sleep under bridges, then there are plenty of people in my own city right now whom I could follow. What is so attractive about Francis and Clare—and virtually all the saints—is their focus: they knew exactly what they wanted from life, and they let nothing distract them from it. It takes focus to create a life that is still worth reading about and emulating eight hundred years after you're dead.

Focus: To Will the One Thing

Kelly's words on inner simplicity, quoted above, are from a chapter called "Holy Obedience." As you may know, the English word "obedience" comes from the Latin verb *ob audire*,[9] meaning "to listen, to hear." So to obey someone is to listen to him or her. The problem most of us have is that we're listening to multiple voices at once. I think of this as the "mall effect," because it's like walking through a shopping mall in which the different stores are all piping in different music; it's disorienting, and there's hardly ever a time when I wouldn't rather shop online or do without.

In a similar way, most of us have different voices coming to us, telling us what we're supposed to do and who we're supposed to be. As Kelly puts it, "We are trying to be several selves at once, without all our selves being organized by a single, mastering Life within us."[10] It's confusing, because all those voices are not a chorus; every one is a soloist and wants our full attention. So we're constantly bombarded with different and even conflicting messages. You'll have your own inventory, but here are a few of mine:

- Don't become a fanatic. (Here in the most "unchurched" corner of the United States, this is a big one.) This whole religion thing is fine in its place, but an hour a week should be enough for anyone. Beyond that, you become eccentric. Much beyond, and you're a freak.
- If you would take some of that time you waste gazing at God (i.e., at nothing—see above about the heathen Northwest) and spend it working out or learning to apply eyeliner, you could be a lot closer to the cultural ideal of attractiveness.
- If you're not going to either lift weights or head to Nordstrom, then at least use that time to get some work done. Productivity is the idol of your tribe. Feed it, or else.

Now, I value exercise and a reasonable level of personal maintenance. I believe in giving my employer an honest day's work for a day's pay. And I'm not likely to start running around waving my hands in the air and shouting "Hallelujah." So I'm willing to go a certain distance with the expectations of my culture. The problem is, cultural expectations are an insatiable beast, and no matter how much we feed it, it's never enough.

In my first year of graduate school, a kindly advanced student sat a bunch of us newbies down and gave us some good advice. He said that it would be physically impossible, given the known limits of time and space, for us to do everything the faculty were going to ask of us. So we were going to have to think about what we valued the most, give that our best efforts, and skate by on the rest. Reflecting on his words years later, I'm impressed by their wisdom. He was really giving us the recipe for sainthood: Figure out what's most important, and focus on that. Put some boundaries around the other demands and keep them in their place, because people who are led in different directions by a host of different voices aren't going to go far in any of them, and one of those voices is God's.

We need focus. Søren Kierkegaard famously wrote that "purity of heart is to will one thing." I'm inclined to think that that kind of pure desire for God, that "singleness of eye" that Kelly spoke of, is not something we can get to just by deciding. A lot of it is grace, God's work of transformation within us. But we can make an effort to focus on what matters, and tune out the babel of voices trying to distract us away from it.

As usual, Jesus shows us the way. I love the way Jesus was always cutting through the layers of trivia people brought to him and getting down to the real issue. Remember the first thing Jesus said when he was first approached by the disciples of John the Baptist? He didn't ask them why they weren't at work, or suggest that they could use a little cardio training. He didn't ask if they were caught up on their chores, if they'd paid their taxes, or whether their accounts were in order. He asked them, "What are you looking for?"[11]

In my mind, this is a pretty funny scene. I imagine the two of them jogging up to Jesus, all full of their intended introduction, and breathlessly launching into it: "We're disciples of John, at least we were, but John said you were the Lamb of God who takes away the sin of the world, not that we know what that means, but anyway John said we should follow you, so here we are and what do you want us to do, and do you have other disciples, and how do you do this whole Messiah thing?" I see Jesus sweeping away all this clutter, fixing his attention on them, and asking: "What are you looking for?"

I think Jesus was really asking them, "What is the deepest desire of your heart? And why are you seeking it here?" The disciples seem to be knocked off balance. Continuing the scene in my mind's eye, I recognize the look on their faces: they're the students who don't know the answer and aren't sure if they're supposed to know the answer, because they haven't done the assigned readings. So their response is evasive: "Ah . . . where do you live?" Frankly, I don't think many of us could answer Jesus' question off the top of our heads. It takes a little reflection to figure out what is the deepest desire of our heart, though if we're ever going to "will one thing," we need to at least try. Jesus is not disappointed in his new students, but responds with a simple invitation: "Come and see."

When I think about the deepest desires of my heart, I begin with the obvious: I desire a good quality chocolate that has no calories and forms a completely balanced diet. Digging a little deeper, I think one of my great desires is for serenity. I'd love to be like Thomas Kelly's description of the person who lives from the "divine Center": "Each one of us can live such a life of amazing power and peace and serenity, of integration and confidence and simplified multiplicity . . . [with] amazing equilibrium of life, amazing effectiveness of living."[12]

Unfortunately, no one who knows me, and certainly no one who's ever lived with me, would mistake me for that person, at least not during my busy season. I don't have a very serene-making job, and during term time I'm more the "pantingly and frantically gasping" type. When I downsized from the tenure-track position to that of senior lecturer, I fantasized that my life would assume a human pace and that there would always be plenty of time for gazing, as well as for family and friends. A decade of reality checks later, I now have a regrettable tendency to fantasize about retirement—regrettable because even early retirement is at least ten years away. Who knows, I may not live long enough to retire, and while that would take care of my inbox and my endless to-do lists, it is a rather drastic solution.

Somewhat less drastic would be a lottery jackpot, or a huge inheritance. But since I don't actually buy lottery tickets, or know anyone who's likely to leave me that kind of money, it seems that God doesn't have a plan for my immediate retirement, and I'm beginning to think I know why: what I'm really doing in my fantasies of life slowing down is grasping at time the way some people grasp at money. A lot of people share my longing for a less frenzied life, one that can be lived at a saner pace, and that is not in itself a bad thing. A lot of the books written on simplicity speak to this very longing, and there's much to be said for it. In my case, however, it's not more time that I need; it's poverty. I don't need more hours to waste on Facebook. What I need is *kenosis*, and my job is as good a source of that as any.

The truth is, I have one of the world's best jobs: teaching six to nine months a year, having a lot of autonomy in the content I teach, getting to introduce young people to new ideas, even new countries when I lead a study abroad program every other year, and being surrounded by good colleagues. Really, most people would kill for a job like mine, and I'm deeply grateful for it. It's just that it's one of those where the work follows you everywhere, and if you don't make a deliberate decision to switch off, it can become all-consuming. It's easy to feel like a hamster on a wheel, going round and round and getting nowhere. It's also easy to burn out when you throw yourself body and soul into a course, and there are always those students who whine about how it was boring or too much work. That's when I start fantasizing about becoming a dog-walker (on sunny days) or a barista (when it's raining sideways).

So like most people who have the luxury of being employed at all, I sometimes feel like my job is a trap, and I could do such amazing things if I could escape it. In reality, however, it's those escape fantasies that are the trap. This was something the early desert hermits understood very well, and a frequent theme of their teaching was the need to resist the seductive idea that things would be better somewhere else. Rowan Williams captures the temptation with painful precision. It's mid-morning, the monk has been weaving the same basket for hours in the rising heat, and is getting bored and restless:

> Is there any progress at all to be seen? Or is this life as featureless as the sand around you? Surely making progress would be more possible elsewhere; after all, in this dead landscape you have no chance to share what you discover, even if you do finally manage

> to discover something. And then, this must be a selfish life: surely there's one of the brothers who'd like a visit, who needs something? And wouldn't I be more useful in the city, anyway? That's where the real need is, and I could supply it so effectively! Anywhere but here, anywhere but now.[13]

Abba Moses has the answer to a hermit who's wondering if there's not some better, deeper, more meaningful life somewhere else: "Sit in your cell, and your cell will teach you everything."[14]

It's not really what we want to hear, is it? Your cell might be your job, a marriage that's grown stale, or a ministry that seems unexciting and unproductive. Anything we long to escape can become a cell. But it's that very boring, featureless place, which feels like a cage, that can become the gate to a secret garden, while running away from it means chasing after a mirage. The desert mothers and fathers understood very well the dangers of a mirage: you can die of heat and thirst pursuing it, but the desert can be hospitable if you stay put long enough to learn its ways.

So what have I learned in my little cell at the University of Washington? First, I've learned that teaching is hard work, especially for introverts like me and many of my colleagues. Introverts are not necessarily shy, but interaction with others tends to take energy from us, whereas extroverts pick up energy in group settings. Lecturing for an hour to several hundred students leaves me drained, the more so because every large class contains at least a few students for whom it's not a good fit and who are not shy about telling you so. As Moses learned in the wilderness, there's nothing worse than trying to lead a bunch of whiners. In fairness, I have to say that students are right to be dissatisfied when "education" consists of sitting in a lecture hall with hundreds of other anonymous units, passively taking in information. I'm working at finding more creative ways to teach large classes, but the economic realities of higher education today mean there's only so much I can do.

For this very reason, I've learned that for me at least, teaching is a path to poverty, a form of *kenosis.* This is because it brings me to the end of my resources. Like any form of poverty, it boils down to having to provide for people and knowing I don't have enough—enough knowledge, enough time, stamina, patience, self-assurance. Just as Clare insisted on the privilege of poverty so her sisters could experience the daily miracle of God's provision, my sense of limitation and inadequacy as a teacher means that every day I teach, I'm forced to begin by asking God to pull it out of the hat again. And each day I end by giving thanks for yet another basket of loaves and fishes.

The *kenosis* I've experienced in my job has helped me find my focus by stripping away distractions and illusions that would have enabled me to stiff-arm God. The fact that I'll never be a famous sociologist is actually liberating, because it means I don't have to spend my life in airports, traveling to meetings with people who want my opinion. More time to gaze. Even better, I've had to give up on a kind of serenity that is illusory, a mirage. This is the calm that's based on knowing that "I've got it covered." There are academics who are unflappable in the classroom because they know that they know everything; at least, they know so much more than their students that it comes to much the same thing.

But when you realize that you don't know much of anything, in the classroom or anywhere, it gives you the focus of someone who's stranded on their rooftop in a flood, watching an approaching helicopter. Remember all those images from Hurricane Katrina? Those people weren't distracted; they weren't thinking about the Olde Worlde architecture of the French Quarter or going for coffee and beignets at the Café du Monde. They had the focus of desperation, and I think that was the focus of Francis, Clare, and all the saints. They knew the one thing they needed to live, and they did not take their eyes off it. Holy people know that obedience means listening, have known it at least since St. Benedict began his famous Rule with the words, "Listen carefully, my son, to the master's instructions, and attend to them with the ear of your heart."[15] It means tuning out the distractions, and listening to the only voice that will tell them how to survive.

We're blessed when life forces us to moments like that. The trick is to string together those moments and turn them into a way of life. I've spent a lot of time on my own small experience of finding a cell in the desert, because it's one of the greatest gifts God can give us. Although it doesn't typically feel like a gift at the time, being stuck in a situation we'd like to change but can't is an experience of inner poverty—as is the experience of being forced into a change we can't understand or control. Both bring us to the end of our resources, and our confidence in our ability to apply them. It is so easy to say that we trust God to supply our needs, while living out of our fantasies of self-sufficiency. The experience of poverty tips us off-center, so that some of what's false within us can splash out, making room for a true self to grow. That spilling out, that *kenosis*, is messy but critically important. It's the way to that purity of heart that wills one thing and one thing only, the purity of heart that prepares us to see God. And if our gaze is a little desperate, it will be all the more focused and steady.

Jesus warned us that the self must die, because he understood that nothing that has not died can live forever. The false self cannot be taken off like a pair of earrings and stored in a box while we wear the true self for a while. God knows that the temptation to wear them again will be irresistible. They have to be destroyed. The false self must be executed so that we can say with St. Paul, "I have been crucified with Christ; and it is no longer I who live, but it is Christ who lives in me."[16]

This connection between the process of *kenosis* and the indwelling of Christ is the key to the mystery. As Carl McColman says, "[M]ystical Christianity is less about attaining unity with God and more about creating the inner emptiness where you can offer God hospitality."[17] Only the excavating process of *kenosis* can clear away the rubble and get us down to the level of the *point vierge*, the hidden chamber where he waits to show us who we really are. Once we stop looking *to* ourselves, then Jesus can help us look *at* ourselves, in the true mirror, which is his own face. There we will see a new creation, and know our own reflection: astonishing, familiar, beloved.

Chapter 7

Imagining the Gaze

> *"Tell me one last thing," said Harry. "Is this real? Or has this been happening inside my head?" Dumbledore beamed at him. . . . "Of course it is happening inside your head, Harry, but why on earth should that mean that it is not real?"*
>
> —J. K. Rowling[1]

Up to now, we've been looking at the wounding and healing of the self: how the self is distorted and hurt, and how our gazing upon God can be part of the process of the self's restoration. In the next two chapters, I want to focus on the gaze itself, and look at the nature and power of contemplative gazing, at variations in how people approach contemplative prayer, and some practical suggestions for how to begin. Let's consider first how and why the sacred gaze has such transformative power.

The Power of the Gaze

Years ago, when we first brought home our eight-week-old golden retriever Abby, I quickly realized I was in way out of my depth. Being Mommy to a furry little bundle of energy and needs was more than I was ready for, so I bought a copy of the classic book *The Art of Raising a Puppy* by the Monks of New Skete. Thirteen years later, I've forgotten most of their advice, but one thing they said intrigued me enough to stay with me all this time. They talked about the importance of eye contact in building a relationship with your dog. Alpha wolves use eye contact to maintain order in the pack, and dogs also respond to it, so the monks provide a set of eye contact exercises you can use to establish yourself as the leader of your "pack."

A prolonged stare will likely be interpreted as a threat by a strange dog—just as it would by a strange human—but gradually increasing eye contact with your own dog will teach him to respect your authority. Abby was such a sweetheart that I really didn't need to work at establishing my dominance over her. But the eye contact exercises serve another purpose, in that they deepen the bond between a dog and her human. Throughout her life, Abby would come and lay her head on the side of the bed, or on my knee, and just gaze at me. I loved her for it, not only because adoration is so easy to take, but because when we gazed into each other's eyes I felt the deep connection between us. She was my brown-eyed girl, and if she's not waiting for me in heaven, there's going to be hell to pay.

Gazing is powerful. Most of us know that intuitively, because we've gazed into the eyes of an infant, a lover, a spouse—even a dog. But it turns out that there's some science behind all this. The psychobiology of love and bonding has identified some of the chemicals in the body that play important roles in the formation of attachments. Oxytocin, also known as the "cuddle chemical," is associated with pregnancy and lactation and is also released during orgasm. It is thought to play a role in the maternal-infant bond as well as in pair-bonding between adults.[2] Vasopressin is also released during sex and lactation, like oxytocin, and may enhance social bonding by stimulating the release of dopamine in the reward centers of the brain.[3]

Interestingly, there are those who claim that "bonding behaviors" such as gazing into another's eyes (as well as skin-to-skin contact, indicating approval with a compliment, providing a treat, kissing, cuddling, and other affectionate and sexual activities) can also stimulate the release of prosocial chemicals like oxytocin, thereby enhancing social bonds.[4] Now, I am not a neuroscientist and am not in a position to provide a critical review of this literature. It seems there's been some interesting research in the area involving animals, and a good bit less using human subjects. So I'm not going to use these studies to argue that the contemplative gaze enhances our attachment to God by setting all these neurochemical processes in motion, but it's an interesting idea. There is research on the neurological effects of meditation that shows, for example, that meditation can promote relaxation by opposing the "fight or flight" response to stress.[5] An interesting book-length exploration of these issues is neurologist and Zen practitioner James Austin's *Zen and the Brain: Toward an Understanding of Meditation and Consciousness.*

Although the field of "neurotheology" is in its infancy, there are some intriguing hints that there may be physiological reasons why gazing at God can draw us into deeper relationship. Thus science is giving us new reasons to trust what Scripture told us long ago: no one can look upon God without being transformed, in ways we cannot anticipate, understand, or control. In a sense, what we gaze at gazes back at us, and changes us, for better or worse. As Nietzsche said, "If thou gaze long into an abyss, the abyss will also gaze into thee."[6]

The advertising industry is well aware of this and forces our gaze continually in the direction of consumer goods, because for people trying to sell us stuff, "consumer" is our primary identity. Because we're so accustomed to this, it's easy to adopt a consumerist mind-set and turn a consuming gaze in every direction. Pornography is a good example of this: the viewer simply consumes; there is no relationship, nothing given in return. My research in sociology has primarily been in the area of tourism, and how people brought together in touristic encounters, especially across cultural, ethnic, and racial divides, see one another. Often what we "see" has been preset for us by the presence in our heads of existing cultural lenses, such as stereotypes and familiar readings of history. These may also be manipulated, deliberately or otherwise, by the tourism industry itself (think of travel brochures that play on clichés of "exotic" locations with "colorful natives").

So we look on people, landscapes, and monuments not with our own eyes but with what John Urry has called the "tourist gaze."[7] Notice how often guidebooks begin coverage of a location with a "must-see" list. This can be very helpful, but it does tend to herd us all in the same directions and predetermine what the travel experience will be. More to the point, when we travel to gaze on people for our own purposes and not for theirs, we become consumers of peoples and cultures. The way most tourism experiences are set up, it is very difficult to get beyond these superficial encounters, even if you want to, as many tourists do. Most of us, if we have the luxury of traveling at all, go for relatively short trips in which our interactions with locals occur at a cash register or on a scripted tour. As with pornography, there is no real relationship and, all too often, little beyond money given in return.

Consumerism is everywhere. There are universities that are now defining education as a "product" and students as consumers. This tends to place faculty in the role of sales clerks, and it's our job to make the customers happy. The internet plays a role in this. I applaud the democratizing quality of the internet, in that it gives ordinary people a voice they didn't have before, but it does mean the phrase "everyone's a critic" is now true in a literal sense. Students in the traditional college age range have grown up posting ratings of everything they encounter, from restaurants to books to makeup, so it's easy for them to bring the same mind-set to their courses. I'm not sure that's healthy, but it's probably not as bad as parishioners who do the same with their pastors. Obviously clergy, like faculty, should be sensitive to the needs of those in their care and accountable for the work they do. But having to put "audience response" first on the priority list never did art any good.

A consumerist mentality means we approach everything with the question, "What's in it for me?" When we bounce from one church to another looking for the magic combination of music, preaching, and liturgy that will make us feel good, we're in it for ourselves. When we look to our teachers for entertainment but not for challenge and growth, we're in it for ourselves. When we visit new places to collect cultural capital rather than be changed by them, we're in it for ourselves. And when we abandon a relationship because we just don't feel the spark anymore, we're out of it for ourselves. The gaze we turn in all these directions is a form of consumption, and the thing about being a consumer is that you control the product you consume. But Nietzsche was right: the abyss looks back, and finds its way in.

It's precisely because the gaze is so powerful that we need to be aware of how we're gazing, and on what. There's a strange little interlude in the story of Israel's exodus from Egypt[8] in which the people have been whining yet again about their rations. So the Lord sends poisonous snakes among them, and many are bitten and die. The people confess their sin and ask Moses to intercede for them, which he does, and the Lord instructs Moses to make a poisonous (or, depending on the translation, a "burning" or "bronze") snake, put it on a pole, "and whenever a serpent bit someone, that person would look at the serpent of bronze and live." Later, Jesus would recall that story and link it to his own: "And just as Moses lifted up the serpent in the wilderness, so must the Son of Man be lifted up, that whoever believes in him may have eternal life."[9] Both are remedies for the death that comes from sin; both are life-giving, and the dying need only *look* to them.

Gazing in the direction of the crucified One gives life, as does the right kind of consuming: "Whoever eats of this bread will live forever; and the bread that I will give for the life of the world is my flesh."[10] The psalmist invites us to "taste *and* see" that the Lord is good.[11] "We become what we behold," as Marshall McLuhan said, and we are what we eat. When what we taste and what we see is Christ himself, we enter into the process of becoming like him: "[W]e will be like him," we are promised, "for we will see him as he is."[12] But gazing is largely a work of the imagination. How do we enter into this, and what are some of the challenges we're likely to face as we try to turn our gaze toward God? People vary considerably in how readily they bring the imagination to prayer, and many of us have had reason to be suspicious of the whole idea. Let's take some time to deal with these concerns before moving on to suggestions for practice, which we'll consider in the next chapter.

The Power of the Imagination

Prayer that makes use of the imagination makes a lot of people nervous, and for good reason. Scripture urges us to be cautious in spiritual matters, where we can easily get in over our heads: "Beloved, do not believe every spirit, but test the spirits to see whether they are from God."[13] One thing that worries people is the danger of subconscious wish-fulfillment. How do I know the experiences I have in prayer are not just me talking to myself, telling myself things I want to hear? I don't want to invent an imaginary friend and call him Jesus. Or maybe the source of what I "see" in my mind's eye, or "hear" with my heart, is even worse than my own subconscious. "Even Satan disguises himself as an angel of light,"[14] although as Carl McColman has observed, the early church fathers taught that it was noise, not silence, that let the demons in. Christians are divided on whether evil spirits exist and, if so, to what extent they can interfere with our prayers. I don't know, but I'm inclined to take the possibility seriously. Better safe than sorry.

What I am certain of is that, whether for psychological or dark spiritual reasons, people have been known to become deeply deluded about spiritual experiences involving the imagination. Marshall Applewhite, who founded the Heaven's Gate movement, imagined that the earth was due to be "recycled," and the comet Hale-Bopp was a means of transport that would carry the faithful to safety. Thirty-eight of his followers ended up dead, having committed suicide in order to board the comet and escape. David Berg, founder of the "Children of God," was an alcoholic who had vivid occult fantasies when he drank, and created such a destructive environment that many who joined his movement were deeply traumatized. The combination of prayer, imagination, and lack of discernment can be deadly, and we'd be foolish to ignore the danger.

But to allow fear to keep us at the shallow end of the spiritual pool is not the answer. If we long to see God face-to-face, the imagination is an important way to get there. As Martin Smith has said, "We behold [Christ's] face through the medium of our imagination, an imagination which is not given over to unbridled fantasies of our own, but one which is disciplined to represent in our hearts the living images and symbols which God has chosen as the alphabet, that palette of colors, of revelation."[15] That the imagination can be abused does not mean it should not be used; we just need to accompany its use with careful discernment. There are some basic principles we can use to keep us from forming our own cults, and I believe that if we follow these, we can steer a safe course between paranoia and naïveté.

First, nothing that happens in prayer should contradict what we learn from Scripture. If Jesus appears to you in a vision and tells you that you're such an emotionally generous person that you can stop making financial donations—sorry, that isn't Jesus. The Bible is plain on this matter: "How does God's love abide in anyone who has the world's goods and sees a brother or sister in need and yet refuses help?"[16] The Word of God isn't going to contradict the word of God, nor is anyone on his side.

Second, the tradition and authority of the church should be your guide. Of course, different factions in the church have disagreed on any number of points over the years, and God will sort us all out someday. But if a little voice comes to you in prayer and says "Jesus wasn't really human, he was just pretending," don't believe it. The church settled that one many centuries ago, and virtually all parts of the church have agreed on the point ever since. God isn't likely to reveal to you that they were wrong.

A third means of discernment is the gift of our reason. A lot of regrettable movements in Christian history could have been avoided if people had used this. For example, Jesus said that no one, not even he himself, knew the day or the hour of his return. And yet, over and over again people have had the bright idea that they knew the date of the Second Coming. If they'd used their heads, they might have figured out that they weren't likely to be better informed on this subject than Jesus. So if things don't make sense or sound bizarre, they should be rejected.

The thing about reason, of course, is that what sounds bizarre to one person may sound perfectly reasonable to another. This is why we need to exercise reason in community, not in isolation. If something significant happens to you in prayer, don't try to figure it out on your own. Get yourself a spiritual director (better yet, get one before you start), or take the matter to your pastor or some other mature believer whose judgment you can trust.

Fourth, if you receive some "message" in prayer that predicts the future, or otherwise reveals something unknown, be very, very skeptical. And then forget about it. God is not going to turn you into a fortune teller. That's not what prayer is about. It's most likely that the Spirit will call to mind things you already know and need to be reminded of, or perhaps a bit of Scripture will prompt you to think about a situation from a different angle. But if God starts telling you who's going to win the next election, get help.

Fifth, Jesus himself gave us the ultimate test: "By their fruits you shall know them."[17] When you've been working with a prayer technique for a while, does it seem to be producing the "fruit of the Spirit" in your life? That is, do you see yourself becoming more loving, joyful, peaceful, patient, kind, generous, faithful, gentle, and self-controlled?[18] Do you see your life increasingly leaning Godward? Is your love for God deepening? Are you having a positive effect on the people around you? These fruits don't show up overnight, but if you're not seeing this kind of change over time, you might need to alter your course. Once again, these things are hard to judge for ourselves; it's impossible by definition to be objective about oneself. So do this work in community, with people you can trust.

Sixth, *ask* God to help. As Karen Kuchan says:

> If you are concerned about what you are experiencing or wonder whether you are making it up, you can ask God to quiet your own voice and any other voices that you might be hearing. You can say something like, "God, please quiet my own voice. I only want to experience what the Spirit who reveals God would like me to experience."[19]

If the potential for self-delusion or deception by others worries you, you should certainly ask God to protect you, but there's no need to become compulsive about it. Nor do these prayers have to be elaborate. If it makes you feel better, go through the whole thing once, telling God exactly what you need. After that, when you begin to pray, just invoke the name of Jesus or the Trinity, or you might start with "Jesus, please protect me." Then proceed with confidence, knowing that "everyone who calls on the name of the Lord shall be saved."[20]

"My sheep hear my voice," Jesus said. "I know them, and they follow me."[21] How do we know his voice? When my husband calls me, he doesn't need to identify himself. I've known him for over twenty years, and I know his voice. As our relationship with Jesus lengthens and deepens, we will become more confident about recognizing his voice. But even then, the principles of discernment will keep us on track.

Finally, accept that you might get it wrong sometimes. Maybe you sense in prayer that you're supposed to approach a problem with a coworker in a particular way, and the ensuing conversation is not a success. This is not catastrophic; sometimes there's just static on the line. Unless you're running around calling yourself a prophet (in which case, according to Deuteronomy 18:20-22, you get the death penalty), then don't worry too much if some insight that comes to you in prayer later seems irrelevant, or even off target. We don't always understand what's going on in the spiritual realm, and sometimes you have to file things away under "to be clarified later." Again, avoid trying to turn the voice of the Spirit into your personal Spidey sense, practice discernment, and then trust that God gives wisdom "generously and ungrudgingly"[22] to all who ask.

We Imagine Differently

We are made in the image of an infinitely complex God, and it's the job of each of us to reflect God's nature back to the world. But we are finite, and no one of us can be more than one small suggestion of the richness of God. This is why we need each other: none of us can contribute more than one tiny piece of the picture. But it's also why we need to be diverse: a jigsaw puzzle in which every piece is sky blue is going to form nothing but sky. As I said in chapter 4, a diverse range of personality types and spiritual styles is one of the strengths of the human species. But it does mean that the ways we use the imagination in prayer are going to be correspondingly diverse.

One of the factors that seems likely to affect whether and how we use the imagination in prayer is gender. I don't want to enter into the debate about whether gender role differences come to us from biology or from the divergent ways in which we're socialized; I personally believe both nature and nurture play a part, but for our purposes here it's really not important. What's important is that while there's certainly much overlap, there do seem to be some differences in the ways women and men tend to pray. Since there are definite differences in the ways we conduct other relationships (again, allowing for individual deviation from the general trends), it could hardly be otherwise.

This is particularly likely to be true of prayer involving the imagination. Highly structured forms of prayer, such as the offices of morning and evening prayer which are read out of a book, probably leave less room for gendered differences than those forms that aim at dialogue, and through it the cultivation of mutuality and exchange. Please don't misunderstand me: I'm not saying that structured prayer is superficial or that it doesn't deepen our relationship with God. The repetitive nature of structured prayers—whether formal public liturgy, or personal devotions such as the Jesus Prayer or the rosary—when practiced over time can effect a profound transformation in the soul. The beauty of such prayers is precisely that they don't require a lot of attention to themselves, so they form an unobtrusive anchor for our restless minds while freeing the soul to move into the presence of God. What I am saying is that if I sit at my kitchen table and imagine having coffee with Jesus, there are a lot more ways in which my being a woman can influence the outcome of that session than if I say the Our Father and read a few psalms.

One of the ways in which my gender may influence prayer using the imagination is whether it will occur at all. Tanya Luhrmann[23] notes that women pray more than men do: according to the 2008 Pew US Religious Landscape Survey, two-thirds of female respondents reported that they pray every day, while less than half of the male respondents do. Based on her own research, Luhrmann believes that this may result from women's greater comfort with using the imagination. One caveat:

Luhrmann's focus here is on evangelicals, which may matter because certain practices that rely on the imagination, such as the Ignatian Spiritual Exercises, are less familiar in that part of the church.

On the basis of ten years of research involving short and lengthy interviews of new and experienced pray-ers, participation in various prayer groups, and analysis of prayer guides and manuals, Luhrmann reached a couple of conclusions. One is that people who learned to "converse" with God, not only to talk to God, but to hear God talk back, learned to do so through the use of their imagination. This often felt silly and contrived at first and was accompanied by a good deal of skepticism, but in time these people came to feel they could distinguish between the voice of God and their own thoughts.

Second, Luhrmann discovered that some people were never able to pray this way and that most of the people who struggled with using the imagination in prayer were men. She administered a test to her subjects that assessed their "capacity and interest in being caught up in the imagination,"[24] and she found that those who had high scores on this test were more likely to pray in ways that were intimate and interactive, and that they were also more likely to be women. She attributes these differences to socialization:

> Our culture raises men to take less joy in the imagination. Men read fewer novels. They play with children less than women do. It is important to understand this difference in socialization because sometimes men who cannot hear God feel like bad Christians. . . . My work suggests that this has more to do with the way our culture teaches them to use their minds than it does with their inherent worth.[25]

Luhrmann concludes that the church should encourage men to develop their imaginations as a means to achieving a richer and more intimate prayer life.

I'm inclined to agree, but gender is only one factor among many that affect whether and how we bring our imaginations into our prayer. Another, as I've already implied, is whether doing so is encouraged and taught in the particular neighborhood of the church that we call home. One of the things I admire about evangelicals and Pentecostals is that they teach people that if they'll get quiet and listen, God will speak. In my experience, it's pretty common in Catholic, Anglican, and mainline Protestant circles for Christians to share with the secular culture the idea that it's normal enough to talk to God, but you should be concerned if God starts talking back. On the other hand, a strength of the older Catholic and Orthodox traditions is the recognition that God sometimes keeps his distance, even from the holiest people. If you've been taught that good Christians hear from God and have a lively sense of his presence, and that's not your experience, it's easy to assume it's because you're a spiritual failure. If your church is not one that holds up Blessed Teresa of Calcutta as a model, you may never realize that you're in pretty holy company.

People are wired differently. As we saw in chapter 4, personalities vary, in ways that can be identified by instruments like the Myers-Briggs Type Indicator, and these differences of personality have implications for our spiritual "styles." In their very helpful book *Prayer and Temperament*, Chester Michael and Marie Norrisey[26] explore the approaches to prayer that best suit different Myers-Briggs types. They note, for example, that Sensing/Judging types (SJs) enjoy "using their sense perceptions and sensible imagination to provide them with passage into the mysteries of Christ's life through the reading of the Scriptures."[27] Intuitive/Feeling types (NFs) are good with both words and symbols, so should be encouraged to keep a spiritual journal, while the Sensing/Perceiving types (SPs) should not, as they primarily relate to God through their sense impressions. They are spontaneous, and are likely to chafe under the structure of the Spiritual Exercises used at an Ignatian retreat but will pray happily with a paintbrush, a musical instrument, or a rake.[28] One prayer suggestion the authors offer to the highly sense-oriented SPs is to "Take your crucifix, look intently at it, feel it, kiss it. In your imagination go back to the first Good Friday."[29]

All of the MBTI types have some capacity for using the imagination, but the ways in which they incorporate it into their prayer will differ. There are people who insist they have "no imagination" to bring to prayer, but this is often the result of a restricted definition of imagination—a failure of imagination, if you will. Suppose I've been to a retreat that revolved around guided meditations. I shut my eyes, try to conjure up a picture, and see . . . nothing. It's easy to understand how I could conclude that I have no imagination, and give up on the whole idea.

But imagination comes in multiple forms.[30] People with a visual imagination will have no trouble envisioning a scene from Scripture and inserting themselves into it, as with the Ignatian Exercises. Others' imaginations are more auditory: they meet God in music, in birdsong, in the drama of a thunderstorm. Still others have a kinesthetic imagination and experience God mainly in physical sensations: God is felt in sunlight on the skin, or plunging into water creates a sense of being wrapped in God's embrace. All of these forms of imagination can yield images—visual, auditory, or kinesthetic—that help us connect with God. I can *see* the place where Jesus comes to meet me; in the sound of the flute in a favorite song I *hear* his voice; the scent of jasmine on heavy summer air makes me *feel* the sweetness of God. Images and imagination can take a variety of forms, any of which can be used to enrich our prayer.

Nevertheless, there are those who just don't experience God in any of these ways. Prayer with images is not the path to which God is calling them, and trying to force it will do more harm than good. Recall that in chapter 5 I mentioned the distinction between "kataphatic" prayer, which is image-based and very emotionally expressive, and "apophatic" prayer, which emphasizes silence and darkness. I agree with those who see these two ways as more complementary than oppositional, yet most of us will find one of them more natural or comfortable than the other. Those of us who have had others try to push us to pray the "other" way have some sympathy with left-handed kids who were forced to write with their right hands. I imagine they felt there was something wrong with them, and people whose spiritual style is more apophatic can likewise feel defective when the God who's supposed to be close and chatty is distant and silent. If that's you, then pick up a book by Thomas Keating, Cynthia Bourgeault, or M. Basil Pennington and see if Centering Prayer is more your style. If that's not you, and you feel open to the use of some form of imagination in prayer, you will find some suggestions in the next chapter for how to begin.

People are wired differently, and this includes our spiritual wiring. Part of learning to love yourself (which we know we're supposed to do, as Christ commanded us to love our neighbor *as our self*) is respecting the way you're designed. "I am fearfully and wonderfully made,"[31] the psalmist exults, which is something Clare of Assisi had learned from a lifetime of gazing into the mirror of Christ. According to witnesses, her final words were, "Blessed are you, Lord, for having created me." How many of us can say that? If we're not there yet, we probably need more time in front of that mirror. Let's get very practical now and consider some ways to begin.

Chapter 8

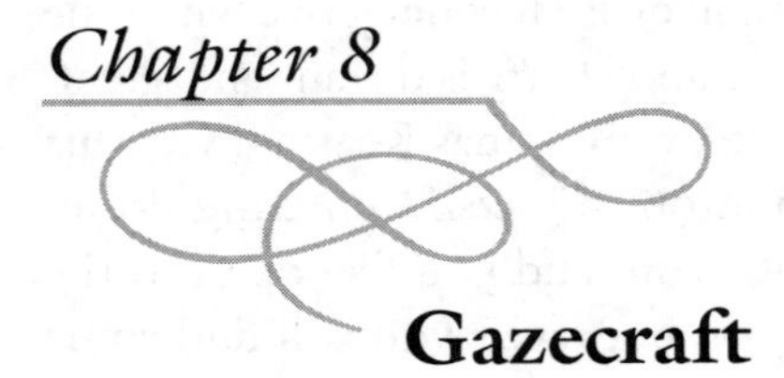

Gazecraft

When You said, "Seek My face,"
My heart said to You, "Your face, Lord, I will seek."
—Psalm 27:8 (NKJV)

If Christ is the mirror in which we can see our true self, and the sacred gaze is a powerful means of healing the self, then the next thing we need to know is how to gaze into that mirror. We may be willing, with the psalmist, to seek God's face, but how do we do it? Where do we look?

We're not on our own here. Over the centuries, as we've seen, devout men and women have found numerous ways of entering into God's presence, and fortunately for us, they've left good maps behind them. But each of our journeys is unique; what St. Bonaventure called "the soul's journey into God" is not like a rail line that runs the same route on the same schedule every day. You don't just take the 8:15 into God from Platform 6. There are signs, to be sure, but ultimately each of us needs to find our own way, guided by the Spirit.

In the last chapter, we saw how differences of gender, personality type, spiritual type, and churchmanship can affect how we pray. What I want to do in this chapter is explore a few methods of prayer that are especially well suited to cultivating a Godward gaze, one that deepens our intimacy with Christ and puts us in a place where he can show us who we really are. Of course, God is sovereign and can work through any method of prayer he chooses. I do think that, for this kind of healing, the gaze is key. But I don't want to be too narrow about what constitutes "gazing"; the sacred gaze is simply a focused attention on God, with an openness to receive whatever is mirrored back to us. As Ilia Delio has put it, to gaze is simply "to penetrate with the heart what is ordinarily missed by the eye."[1] This can happen any number of ways, and I can cover only a few of them here.

In this chapter, then, I will begin with one of the better known methods of preparing for contemplation, *lectio divina*, and show how *lectio* itself, and two variants of it that make extensive use of the visual and auditory forms of imagination, can provide a way of seeking the face of Christ. These are ways of cultivating the contemplative gaze that I have found very helpful, so I will focus on describing them in some detail. But they are hardly the only ways, so the remainder of the chapter will look at some other methods of prayer and consider how they might focus our attention on God and contribute to the healing of the self.

Part of the gift of human creativity is our endless ingenuity in exploring the uncharted terrain of the soul. The methods described here are not meant to be exhaustive or definitive; they are just examples of approaches that have proved helpful to me and to others. The point is for you, under the Spirit's guidance, to find the path God has prepared specifically for you. Once you have experimented with some different methods of prayer, ideally with the help of a good spiritual director, it's good to settle on one and stick with it for a while. As the saying goes, if you're looking for water, it's better to dig one hole six feet deep than six holes one foot deep.

Lectio Divina

One of the oldest ways of deep praying in Christian history, which has had a renaissance in our own day, is *lectio divina*—

literally, "holy reading." At one time *lectio* was practiced by virtually all Christians, but eventually laypeople (and even clergy and religious) were discouraged from entering into deep prayer and told to confine themselves to vocal prayer.[2] (This may be where people started "saying their prayers" instead of praying.) The practice of *lectio divina* was kept alive, however, by Benedictines and other monastics and has been recovered and widely taught in recent years.[3]

Lectio divina is prayer that depends on deep listening, principally to the words of Scripture, though any text that speaks to the soul can be used. It begins with *lectio* (reading; pronounced LEK-see-oh): quiet, attentive, and reverent listening for the "still, small voice" of God in the text. No scanning the page, no rubbing it with your eyes; this is reading that requires us to go slowly and repeat several times. Nor is this the careful reading one associates with study. When we study Scripture, we try to understand the historical context, we may investigate key terms in the original language, we may be looking for theological significance, or we may be preparing a sermon or a lesson. With *lectio*, we are not so much looking for "what the Bible says"; rather, we are listening for what the Spirit is saying to us individually, in this moment, through these words. The goal is not systematic theology or exegesis but communication that is intimate, loving, and personal.

Incidentally, many people find that committing Scripture to memory helps accomplish something very like this, in that the Spirit is able to draw from the store of remembered verses to bring to mind the one that's right for the moment. You might call this "*lectio*-to-go."

When it seems that particular words are speaking to us, inviting closer attention, we move to the next step, which is *meditatio* (meditation). We spend time with a particular passage, a phrase, even a single word, and let it take root deep within. Mary is our model here: we don't need a lot of commotion and commentary; we just ponder the words in our heart. There they will sink in deep, and not return void but accomplish the purpose for which God sent them.[4] If God's purpose is to heal a broken sense of self, it's not hard to see how that healing could be advanced through meditation on a passage like Zephaniah 3:17 (Complete Jewish Bible):

> *Adonai* your God is right there with you,
> as a mighty savior.
> He will rejoice over you and be glad,
> he will be silent in his love,
> he will shout over you with joy.

The next stage is *oratio* (prayer), where we talk with God about whatever is on our hearts: the content of our meditation and anything else. This is dialogue, though, so we listen as well as talk, confident that "My sheep hear my voice."[5] *Oratio* includes the prayer of oblation, offering the self to God. We open ourselves to God's purpose and pray that it might be fulfilled in us, that we might cooperate and not obstruct. This is a loving, joyful (or possibly agonizing and fearful) surrendering of our own will into the hands of a trustworthy God.

Finally, we come to *contemplatio* (contemplation), where we cease all activity and simply rest in the presence of God. There is no need for words at this point; they will only get in the way. All the preceding steps have stripped away the distractions and the busyness of our minds and hearts, and there is nothing left but the sacred gaze. We have listened, we have offered ourselves, and we have determined—hopefully, fearfully, probably both—to hold nothing back. And now, with naked soul, we hold that gaze as long as we can, and as we hold it, we are known, loved, healed.

It's not necessary to go through each of these steps every time, nor do we have to be rigid about their order or duration. Descriptions of *lectio divina* all move in essentially the same direction, but the steps often vary. I could easily imagine the prayer of oblation coming at the conclusion of contemplation, for example, and contemplation itself might be very brief: just a couple of seconds that seem to contain time and eternity. As with any method of prayer, it's worth paying attention to the guidance and instruction of people who know it intimately through long experience. But then ask the Spirit to guide you, and go where you're led. Remember, this is your journey, not theirs.

Lectio divina is a time-honored method that has brought many a seeker to the face of Christ. But I would like to look at two variations on this theme, two other forms of prayer that have been central to my own spiritual formation. These are *visio divina* and *audio divina*, which make particular use of the visual and auditory forms of imagination. I practiced both of these for years before I discovered that some very fine teachers of prayer had given names to them, and worked out both the implications of each method and how it could be taught to others. So although I sort of stumbled into these techniques on my own (or, one hopes, under the Spirit's direction), I am greatly indebted in the pages that follow to Karen Kuchan's book *Visio Divina: A New Prayer Practice for Encounters with God*[6] and two websites on *audio divina*, one by Mary Terry Rankin and the other by Christine Valters Paintner.[7] I highly recommend these writers for more information on the techniques I describe below, which are nevertheless described according to my own experience of them.

Visio Divina

There are a variety of forms of prayer that are visually based. Perhaps praying with icons or other sacred pictures or objects is the most obvious example, and we'll explore some of those methods later. One variation on this theme that may not be so obvious is praying with moving icons, that is, with film. I've mentioned elsewhere[8] that the 2003 film *The Gospel of John*, with Henry Ian Cusick in the role of Jesus, is my favorite Jesus movie. The script is the gospel alone, nothing added and nothing (except for the odd "and then he said") removed, so that to watch it is to "read" the gospel.[9] I spent several years watching some part of this three-hour film virtually every day, and it both deepened my knowledge of John's gospel and dramatically changed my prayer. Seeing a story is different from reading it, and it's worth trying this out to see how it affects you.

Visio divina takes this idea a step further and works a kind of Ignatian twist on it. Ignatius of Loyola taught people to imaginatively enter into scenes in the Scriptures: Picture the Sermon on the Mount and imagine you're in the crowd listening to Jesus. What's the weather like that day? What's the mood of the people? How do you feel when Jesus says, "Blessed are those who mourn"? Do you feel like he may be seeing into your heart? Just as Ignatian meditation asks people to visualize a scene like this, in *visio divina* we imaginatively create scenes, but they needn't be based in Scripture.[10] Before going any further, though, let me explain how I came to pray this way.

Some years ago, I saw a film called *The Perfect Stranger*, based on David Gregory's novel *Dinner with a Perfect Stranger*. In the film, a woman named Nikki (a man in the book) receives a mysterious invitation to dine with Jesus Christ. She's skeptical, even hostile, but before the evening is finished, Jesus has won her over and she is changed. The film was produced by Kelly's Filmworks, which went on to do several more full-length films, such as one in which Nikki's daughter sits next to Jesus on a cross-country flight, and a series of shorts in which Jesus meets a variety of people who don't at first know who he is.

The quality of these films ranges from so-so to fairly cringeworthy, but I was fascinated by the premise. What if I sat next to Jesus on a flight? What if he showed up in my office after a discouraging class session or was waiting in my kitchen at the end of a long day? What would he say to me, and how would I respond—once I recovered consciousness?

I started redoing the films in my head. One of the things that particularly troubled me about them was that when people finally realized it really was Jesus, their response seemed a lot more muted than I'd expect in a surprise encounter between a human being and the divine Logos, even in high-top sneakers. A twinkle of recognition in the eye, a "Dude, where've you been?" just didn't seem to do the situation justice. I imagined how I would react. It seemed to me that the first thing I'd do would be to fall at his feet weeping. And then we'd have some talking to do: me confessing that I'd screwed up everything beyond repair, and he—well, what would he say?

This is where the healing came in. I tried this out over and over, for months, then years. And every time I looked at him, all I could see in his face, all I could hear in his voice, was compassion, and an image of myself that transcended all the things about me that seemed broken. I assumed this was wish-fulfillment: after all, I really wanted him to not be angry at me, so of course I would set up scenes in my head in which Jesus was forgiving. What I didn't notice at first was that my conscience was actually becoming more sensitive, not less. But increasingly, when I realized I'd missed the mark somehow, I didn't fixate on what that said about *me*. Instead, I felt deep remorse for what I had done to *him*. So instead of becoming ever more self-centered or self-indulgent, I developed a growing desire to become the person he was showing me in the mirror.

It took a long time to believe that the image reflected in the face of Jesus was really me. I was every bit as skeptical and hostile as Nikki in the film: I challenged; I questioned; I didn't believe any of it. Yet I kept at it, and while I did, I practiced all the methods of discernment I described in the last chapter to determine whether it was safe to believe any of this. Every source and every person, including people living and dead whom I knew to be holy and wise, pointed me in the same direction: Trust this. This is one of God's ways of speaking to you.

I knew about "guided meditation," in which one person gently leads another through a scene in which they encounter God, revisit troubling situations from the past, and so on. This is a common enough technique in the retreat and spiritual direction settings, as well as in Christian and even secular counseling. I suppose what I'm describing is a kind of do-it-yourself guided meditation. But as I experimented with it, I noticed that while I tended to begin in an active role by setting the scene, increasingly it would take on a life of its own. My role became more and more passive as I simply allowed the scene to play out, sometimes taking unexpected turns. As with *lectio divina*, in *visio divina* periods of active communication often end in quiet, loving attentiveness. What begins with a particular text or scene and moves into meditation often ends in contemplation: the simple communion of a soul alone with God.

Another thing I noticed about these sessions was that they would sometimes produce insights that were real "Aha!" moments. That is, they initially took me by surprise but, on reflection, seemed right on target. I could also see, with the help of trustworthy mentors, that I was experiencing real spiritual growth and even being somewhat useful to others. By their fruits you shall know them.

All of this growth may have brought me up to the point where you began; if so, I'm delighted for you. Some of us have more to learn than others. But the point is that I did grow, and *visio divina* was a powerful catalyst for that growth. The other important point, however, is that the transformation I experienced through *visio divina* has been heavily weighted toward *healing*, particularly healing of my sense of self. In these encounters with Christ, he mirrored back to me a view of myself I had not suspected. As I've said, it took me a long time to believe in it. But this is something Karen Kuchan emphasizes repeatedly: the power of *visio divina* lies in its capacity to bring us in touch with the love of God, which will inevitably have a healing and transformative effect on us at the deepest levels of the soul.

Audio Divina

Anyone who's ever been moved by a piece of music knows that music can touch the soul in a way that's unique and powerful.

I would bet that most believers pray to music from time to time without really thinking about it, if only in church. But when you do think about it, and pray with music intentionally, it can be like a greased slide that lands you right in the lap of God.

There are three ways I can think of by which music can take us into prayer; perhaps you can think of others. First, there is music that can simply still the spirit and allow us to mark a particular time and place as sacred. Of course, in one sense, we are always in God's presence, and the longer we hang around God, the more we realize that prayer is going on all the time; all times and places are sacred. Still, it's important to step out of our routines and set aside time to focus exclusively on God, to "seek God's face," as the psalmist says. Music that is quiet and meditative, perhaps even gently repetitive, can be the auditory equivalent of lighting a candle or reading a passage of Scripture. The Spirit invites us to "be still, and know that I am God."[11] Gregorian and Taizé chants can be excellent for this, as can any music that is fairly simple and restful.

A variant of this is to use music to help clear away distractions so you can focus on a particular theme, especially when that theme is a difficult one. I could devote the rest of this book to the things that annoy me about the kitschy 1970s film *Jesus Christ Superstar*. But I often listen to the Gethsemane scene during Holy Week, because even though the theology is deeply flawed, the raw emotion brings home to me the fact that this was a *man*, struggling with his fear and his desire to run away from a degree of physical and spiritual suffering beyond my imagining. So I just ignore the sketchy theology and let the music draw me into the agony of that moment.

But music is so personal. My playlist is my psalter, and no one else's. I could tell you about the selections that have been useful to me, but I'm a middle-aged woman with pretty strange musical tastes, and especially if you're a decade or two older or younger, my choices will probably not resonate with you. Experiment; discover the pieces that do work for you. If you're not sure where to begin, there is a list of suggestions at www.audiodivina.com.

A second way in which music has become prayer for me is when a piece of music that seems to convey a particularly apt message finds its way into my head and won't leave. We've probably all had the experience of "earworms," those tunes that play over and over in your head until you want to poke out your eyes with a stick. I don't know why, but it's usually the most awful songs this happens with, the ones you never want to hear again even once, let alone a hundred million times over the course of a few days. (Remember "Macarena"?)

But sometimes I wake up in the morning with a song in my mind that has just the words I need for that day. It's like having my own soundtrack, and the lyrics convey the bit of wisdom I'll need to get through the day's challenges without losing my mind. A song that lifted my spirits over a rocky little section of the path was "Count on Me" by Jefferson Starship. (Did I mention I'm middle aged?) The curious thing is that it's very often songs I never really listened to, by bands I never liked, that end up playing this role. One year I spent five months abroad and traveled from England to Italy, France, Spain, Ghana, Hungary, Poland, Germany, Ireland, and Wales. I was struck by how, in all these places—some familiar, many not—I always managed to find a church where I could feel a sense of *home*, some place where I could rest awhile in the house I'd grown up in.

Throughout my wanderings that year, I kept hearing snippets of a song by a band that must have been stoned when they named themselves Badfinger. They were not a band I listened to in my youth, but during those months of travel, I kept hearing a phrase from a song of theirs that I later discovered was called "No Matter What." When I finally was exasperated enough to Google the lyrics, I discovered these words: "No matter where you go / There will always be a place / Can't you see it in my face, girl?"[12]

A song like that is a gift, and about all you can do is be alert and try not to miss it when it comes. But when you do come across a piece that has special meaning for you, there is a third way it can be used in prayer. The soundtrack to the *Gospel of John* film was done using instruments from the time of Jesus, and while some of the tracks include singing in Aramaic, the language Jesus would have spoken in everyday life, most of them are instrumental, which is probably best for this purpose.

I found several of the pieces on this soundtrack hauntingly evocative and spent a lot of time with them, just listening. Eventually, though, as I listened each one became a musical version of *visio divina* by creating a scene in which I encountered Jesus. This form of *audio divina*, that is, doing *visio divina* to music, is particularly powerful because of the ability of music to focus our attention and drive away distractions. Music, like pain, forces us to live in the present moment. We all know how difficult it is to recall one tune while we're listening to another. Music can be an excellent corrective to our compulsive multitasking.

Of course, the power of music to create an imaginative experience for the listener is not incidental; it's what much music is for. Tchaikovsky's *1812 Overture* is meant to bring the audience into the experience of battle. Brahms's *German Requiem* captures the dread and grief associated with death; frankly, the piece scares the hell out of me, which is just the point. The very power of music to suck us into an experience means that we should choose music for prayer carefully. It's probably best to use pieces that either have no lyrics or have lyrics that are unobtrusive, perhaps in a language you don't know. You don't want the experience overly defined for you; it's best to allow space for the scenario to unfold as the Spirit leads.

Setting the Scene

Whether you are going to begin with film, text, music, or just the divine gift of a creative mind, the first thing you'll need to do is set the scene. Where will you encounter Jesus today? (As an aside, the more visual of these methods of prayer tend to be Christocentric; if you're going to imagine meeting God face-to-face, it helps a lot if he *has* a face.) You might want to ask him where he'd like to meet you, and if nothing springs to mind feeling "right," then just ask for guidance and proceed. Is there a place where a lot of your emotional energy is centered at the moment? If you're having trouble at work, that might be a good place to begin. If you're sick, maybe you can envision Jesus sitting at your bedside. Or maybe you'd like to meet him in a favorite place, like a beach or a garden. I've found that photographs of beautiful places often become an invitation; I've come across some beautiful settings in gardening magazines and on Facebook pages such as *Green Renaissance* and *A Room with a View*. Once you've been praying this way for a while, if you can't seem to figure this part out, take the advice a spiritual director once gave me: seek him where you last saw him.[13]

Once you've decided on the setting, how do you first see him, and what sorts of feelings does that arouse within you? Are you remorseful? Confess what's on your heart, and then see how he responds. Maybe you're filled with awe: begin with praise. Maybe you're overcome with emotion and experience the "gift of tears"; let him hold you close while you cry it all out. Or perhaps you need to talk over a situation before you can come to rest in his presence. Having prayed for the Spirit's guidance, you can simply allow the scene to unfold, confident that "When you search for me, you will find me; if you seek me with all your heart, I will let you find me, says the Lord."[14]

Scripture does speak of times when we don't seem able to find him. The woman in the Song of Songs knew something of the pain of searching for someone greatly desired who has disappeared: "I opened to my beloved, but my beloved had turned and was gone. My soul failed me."[15] I've written elsewhere about the experience of spiritual darkness, when God seems absent.[16] These times can be agonizing, but they play a critical role in our spiritual development. When we feel abandoned and engulfed in darkness, it's important to keep two things in mind. First, there's a difference between *feeling* close to God and *being* close to God. Second, the darkness itself is saturated with God. Even if you don't feel it, you know that God is omnipresent; do you think the spot you occupy at this moment is the one and only exception to that? There are times when you have to go with what you know rather than what you feel.

Many of the greatest masters of prayer over the centuries have borne witness to the truth that it is in the times of darkness that God's work within us is most profound, though obscure.[17] The best thing we can do at those times is to wait patiently and trustingly for God to do this work.[18] Part of what God does during episodes of darkness is to teach us that pleasant feelings are not the goal of the spiritual life; God is the goal. For some people, such as Mother Teresa, these periods can go on so long that they become a way of life. For most of us, however, they are seasons we pass through. While they last, they can fill us with pain and confusion. But competent spiritual direction, and the knowledge that this is a positive process, can help us get through them and emerge with a much deeper intimacy with God.

Other Visual Ways of Gazing

Creating scenes in which we encounter Christ is not the only visual way to cultivate a contemplative gaze. Clare invited Agnes of Prague to gaze into the mirror of the Crucified, and certainly gazing at a crucifix is one way to focus our attention on Christ, the mirror in which Clare said Agnes would find herself. Similarly, those at home in the Catholic tradition may find praying before the Blessed Sacrament to be a powerful means of fixing the mind and heart on Christ. But Evelyn Underhill suggested that contemplation could begin with fixing one's gaze on a stone. It's important not to get too hung up on technique, or whether we're "doing it right." After all, we're talking about approaching God here; who among us really knows what they're doing? But Jesus promised that if we asked for a fish, we will not be given a snake. If fallible human parents know how to give good gifts to their children, "how much more will the heavenly Father give the Holy Spirit to those who ask him?"[19] So don't be afraid to experiment; trust that the Spirit will be your guide.

I want to just mention two other visual forms of prayer in which we can encounter Christ. One is the use of icons, which has been with the church for many centuries. Prayer with icons is well known to Orthodox Christians but has become increasingly popular of late among those of us from the Western traditions. If you want to explore this type of prayer, I would urge you to get a good, basic introduction such as Jim Forest's *Praying with Icons*, a modern classic that is helpful for beginners. One of the first things you'll learn is that icons are not "art"; that is, they're not created for their aesthetic appeal. Icons are "written" (not painted) to serve as windows or doors we can gaze through into the realm of the sacred.

Icons depict all sorts of subjects, but for our purposes, you'll probably want to start with an image of Jesus. The genre of "Christ Pantocrator" portrays Christ risen, glorified, and all-powerful. Some of these can be a little intimidating, while others are more gentle; choose carefully! There is also an icon of the resurrection in which Christ is bringing Adam and Eve up from the place of the dead. Rowan Williams points out that these are not the youthful, innocent faces we associate with our primal parents in the garden. These are the faces of fallen people grown old:

> Their faces are lined by suffering and experience, by guilt, by the knowledge of good and evil, scarred by life and by history. This is Adam and Eve having lost their innocence—the Adam and Eve who are of course ourselves. . . . The resurrection is not about the wiping out of our history, pain or failure, it is about how pain and failure themselves—humanity marked by history—may yet be transfigured and made beautiful.[20]

What Archbishop Williams is doing here is modeling for us how, in gazing even at images of our fallenness, we can discover our own transfiguration in Christ. This is a healing gaze.

The other visual form of prayer that I wanted to mention is to simply gaze into the faces of people around us and use our imagination to see Christ in them. This approach was really taught to us by Jesus himself: when he said that whatever we do to the least of his brothers and sisters we do to him, he was asking us to *see* him in them. Of course, we need to be careful in our interpretation of what we see mirrored back to us in those faces. Even the most gracious overtures can be met with hostility, and when they are, it doesn't mean we're being rejected by Christ himself! You might even consider trying this out with photographs; certainly you can get away with staring at them longer than you can with live humans. Look at those faces attentively, and you'll come to see Christ in them. Look a bit longer, and you may see yourself in them. Keep looking, and you may even discover that you're seeing them and yourself with the eyes of Christ, with the compassion of Christ.[21] If you can't seem to find the face of Christ in a person, particularly someone you dislike, try praying for that person for a while. Focusing on their need and vulnerability may soften your feelings for them. With time and practice, the faces of the most difficult people can become icons for us, "windows into heaven." And if you look at a window just right, you can see your own reflection in it too.

Gazing with the Body

There are lots of ways that those with a more kinesthetic imagination can cultivate a contemplative gaze. A very simple one is to take a walk, go for a run, paddle a kayak, or sit on a bench, in a beautiful place. Consider your surroundings, and what it says about you that God created such a beautiful world for your enjoyment. If not yours, then whose? It didn't have to be this way; presumably God could've made the world ugly, but he didn't. And it is no more a gift to you than it is to others, but it is also no less. I once had the immense good fortune to be on a beach in the Bahamas. The water was so beautiful I thought my heart would explode, and when I dove into it, I felt I was immersed in God himself. And this was a God who'd created such beauty just for our delight. The color and clarity of the water, the brightness of the fish, the sound of gentle waves—it was so sensuous, such a feast for the senses. At the same time, it was a feast for the spirit and brought me face-to-face with the sheer generosity of God.

There's a scene in the movie *Chariots of Fire* where the Olympic sprinter Eric Liddell tells his sister Jenny, "I believe God made me for a purpose. But he also made me fast. And when I run, I feel his pleasure." *I feel his pleasure.* If you're an athlete, or a dancer, when you're doing what you do best, do you feel God's pleasure? That is the kinesthetic imagination at work. When your body feels healthy and strong, capable of amazing things, can you look to God and sense his delight? Your body may not always be healthy and strong, and someday you'll probably lose your ability to do amazing things with it. But you will always be the person to whom God gave that talent, the person whose grace and power pleased him. Can you feel his pleasure?

A kinesthetic imagination doesn't require youth, strength, and grace, however. Maybe you've got a way with pastry, and you can feel that divine delight when you turn out a pie crust that floats up to the angels. Or you love gardening, and a perennial border you planned explodes into glorious bloom. But it doesn't even require exceptional talents to tap into that sense of God's deep approval. If you're looking for it, you can feel it when you're rocking a sleeping baby and feeling its breath on your face, or cuddling a dog you've saved from being destroyed. The number of ways we can employ a kinesthetic imagination to connect with God is unlimited, but this path requires that we be intentional. A well-run race can help us feel God's pleasure, or it can be a display of ego and a prop for the false self. The difference lies in where our attention is fixed—that is, on the direction of our gaze.

The Healing Gaze

Virtually any form of prayer that fixes my attention on Christ can help me get to know him better, but how does all of this help me get to know myself? Where does the healing of my own identity come in? There are at least two ways I know of by which this kind of prayer can transform my sense of self. The first lies in Jesus' responses to me. Remember the looking-glass self: I come to know who I am as I see myself mirrored in others with whom I interact. When you interact with Jesus, what is his stance toward you? Does he seem angry, judgmental, or disappointed? Or do you sense tenderness and compassion? Perhaps he agrees that something in your life needs to change, but does he condemn you for it or see it as part of a bigger picture?

The idea that God places my faults in a larger context was something I learned when, in my prayer, my attention was continually drawn back to my dog, Abby. Abby the blessed, Abby the beloved, the late and much lamented, she was the embodiment of all that a golden retriever should be: a true lovehound. She wore her fur like a full-body halo, but she did have one bad habit: she liked to eat poop. Her poop, other dogs' poop, cat poop—Abby was entirely undiscriminating. It took "dog breath" to a whole new level, gave her occasional parasites that freaked me out, and was generally a habit I did not admire. But it didn't make me love her less, and if she hadn't done it, I wouldn't have loved her more. She was just Abby, and I loved her. And Jesus gently taught me that my metaphorical poop-eating came to much the same thing in his eyes. Yes, we'd work on those things, and they'd all be overcome, in this life or the next. But I could still be his beloved companion, as Abby had been mine.

The second way in which healing of the self can occur in prayer is based on a startling truth: you are invited to your own transfiguration. It is the destiny of each of us to share, to participate, in the glory that was revealed in Christ on Mount Tabor. Skeptical? I don't blame you, but this idea comes up again and again in Scripture. We get hints, for example, in the psalms: "Look to him, and be radiant; so your faces shall never be ashamed."[22] But let's begin with Jesus himself. His transfiguration, as we have seen, is the climactic moment in the Synoptic Gospels, the event that reveals his true identity. In John's gospel, in his prayer to the Father before his arrest, he prays for his disciples, and "not only on behalf of these, but also on behalf of those who will believe in me through their word"—that's us—"The glory that you have given me I have given them."[23]

Remember what St. Paul said: "And all of us, with unveiled faces, seeing the glory of the Lord as though reflected in a mirror, are being transformed into the same image from one degree of glory to another."[24] The first letter of John echoes the theme: "Beloved, we are God's children now; what we will be has not yet been revealed. What we do know is this: when he is revealed, we will be like him, for we will see him as he is."[25] In both of these texts, the promise is that we will be transformed into the image of Christ in glory, and this transformation is effected precisely by *gazing* on his glory.

This theme has been central to Christian theology in the East; it's a pity that Western Christendom hasn't paid it more attention.[26] In Orthodox thought, what the disciples witnessed in the transfiguration was the deified flesh of Christ, radiant with uncreated light. This was no natural light; we're told that Jesus' face "shone like the sun,"[27] and yet the people waiting below saw nothing. And no wonder: they had not been through the purifying ascent that would prepare them to see Christ's face. But for Orthodox Christians, the saints are those who have attained the Beatific Vision, which is the light from the deified flesh of Christ that shines into their eyes, into their very selves.

Saint Symeon the New Theologian (d. 1022) used the image of iron in the fire to show the way in which we are meant to take that uncreated light into ourselves and be transformed, transfigured, by it. The iron becomes incandescent in the fire, infused with fire; indeed, it becomes "all fire," as Abba Joseph counseled Abba Lot.

When Jesus spoke of giving his glory to those who would believe in him through the testimony of the apostles, this is something of what he meant. He would ignite us with his own fire, and, like the bush on Sinai, we would burn with it and not be consumed. Likewise, Christ's resurrection reveals his ultimate intention for us. The resurrection of Christ is not a one-off event that's nice for him but has nothing to do with us. Paul insists that "Christ has been raised from the dead, the *first fruits* of those who have died."[28] He goes on to say: "So it is with the resurrection of the dead. What is sown is perishable, what is raised is imperishable. It is sown in dishonor, it is raised in glory."[29]

Well, so what? All this talk of transfiguration, resurrection, and glorification may seem a long way off, and no great consolation when you feel like a loser in the present moment. And the present moment is all we have. But remember that God dwells in eternity, and can see all of this fulfilled in you right now. So while the first way God can heal our sense of self through prayer is by responding to us in ways that suggest compassionate love, the second way I would propose is this: Try asking Jesus to show you a glimpse of yourself as he sees you. As you visualize a face-to-face encounter with him, what would happen if he led you up to a mirror? What might you see there? I don't know what you would see there, but my look into that mirror has changed everything. Here's Paul again:

> So we do not lose heart. Even though our outer nature is wasting away, our inner nature is being renewed day by day. For this slight momentary affliction is preparing us for an eternal weight

> of glory beyond all measure, because we look not at what can be seen but at what cannot be seen; for what can be seen is temporary, but what cannot be seen is eternal.[30]

A middle-aged woman whose flesh is rotting on the bone is what I see when I look into a natural mirror, but when I gaze into the mirror of Christ, the view is very different. Is what's happening in *visio divina* "real"? At one level, no. You can meditate all day on Jesus in the kitchen doing your dishes, but when you open your eyes, they'll still be in the sink. And yet, the self that Christ reveals to me is the deeper reality, even now. Contemplation is about stepping out of the world of surface appearances and illusions and into eternity in the presence of God. The eternal reality is that each of us bears a "weight of glory" that would dazzle us like the sun if we looked straight into it now. But like the sun, seeing by its light makes everything else more clear.

Let us ask to be shown a glimpse of that light. God may choose to reveal it to us as bright light or as "radiant darkness," the light so bright that it blinds us and leaves us in the dark with nothing but trust. Either way, we can be sure of this: we look to a God who is infinite and loves us without limits. We can use our imagination freely, because both the power and love of Christ are "abundantly far more than all we can ask or imagine."[31] Whatever we dare to imagine about God and his love for us, the reality will always be better, deeper, more.

Chapter 9

Active Contemplation: The True Self in the World

If we are to love our neighbors, before anything else we must see our neighbors.

—Frederick Buechner[1]

It's time to return to an important question: Why is all this work on the self, on finding my true self, not selfish? Isn't going on a voyage of discovery that's all about Me just a little narcissistic? The answer is no, precisely the opposite. Discovering the true self is essential because *the false self cannot love.* It's too consumed with its own needs. This doesn't mean that people who haven't gone in search of their true self are incapable of love, far from it. But real love comes from the truest part of ourselves, and growing deeper in love—the kind of heroic, sacrificial love Christ calls us to—means that the false self must increasingly be displaced by the true. And the false self will not give up gracefully; Jesus told us that it has to die. Only then can the person he is calling each of us to be grow up in its place. This is the paschal mystery again: nothing that has not died can live forever, and to nothing does this apply more fully than the self.

So the false self must die, because it is incapable of fulfilling the commandments to love God and to love our neighbor as our self. We seek to live from a true self so that our lives can be about love. But what is love, exactly?

Love Is the Point

You're probably familiar with the fact that ancient Greek had several words for love: *agape* (self-giving, unconditional love), *eros* (passionate love, attraction), and *philia* (fraternal love, friendship), as well as *storge* (affection).[2] English is generally a rich language with lots of choices for expressing a given idea, but in this area we are comparatively poor. We have only the one word *love*, so we work it awfully hard: I love my husband; I love God; I love my iPad; I love Indian food. If the number of pop songs written about a concept can be taken as an indication of its cultural importance, love is right up there, so you'd think we'd have a better vocabulary for it. Of course, in many of those songs, "love" is really a euphemism for "sex." My husband pointed out to me years ago that when a singer says, "Oooh baby, give me your love," he's not really asking for her undying devotion. Probably the devotion of an hour or so will suffice.

Another indicator of our confusion about love is how often people think they can't love someone they don't like. If "love" is just "like" only more so, then you can't, really. But if we were to take *agape* as our model, then whether we liked someone would be irrelevant. The test of whether we loved them would be whether we were prepared to put their interests before our own. So the next time someone gazes into your eyes and says, "I love you," you might want to stop them and ask for clarification.

These questions came up for me the first time I read Cornel West's now classic book, *Race Matters*.[3] West did an interesting and important analysis of some of the challenges facing the African American community, ranging from very practical matters such as the need for leadership to more philosophical ones such as the threat of nihilism. It was making a lot of sense to me, and I was eager to know what sorts of solutions he'd propose. In the end, his answer was: love. "Love?" I thought, "*love*?" I was fresh out of graduate school, still in love with social science, and was looking for something a little more, shall we say, policy oriented. But Cornel West is not a social scientist; he is a philosopher and ordained minister, and I should've known better. I laid the book aside and forgot about "love" for a while, until I read another of West's books, an earlier one called *Prophetic Reflections*.[4]

Out of West's discussion in this book I draw an understanding of love that has three main components. It begins with a commitment to the notion of *imago Dei*, that is, to the idea that every human being bears the image of God. Once the divine image is *seen* in the other, then responsibility for the other's welfare is implicitly accepted; I *am* my brother's keeper. I would add that it is entirely possible to begin from a secular commitment to the notion that all human beings are of equal value, but for believers, to begin with the divine image is especially powerful. Either way, if we accept that others have a claim on us because of who they are, rather than what they do or what they've earned, then we will not make it our business to draw distinctions between those who deserve a good life and those who don't.

Having accepted the obligation that comes from our shared humanity, West suggests that our next responsibility is *analysis*. That is, if those who are made in God's image are suffering, we need to have the intellectual integrity to try to understand why. It's easy to see how important this is if we make it concrete and think about how we treat those we know we love versus those we probably don't. If my best friend's marriage breaks up, I can expect to spend a lot of time in conversations with her about what happened. We'll probably try out numerous hypotheses and struggle to make sense of it: Was she inadequate somehow? Was there someone else? Is her ex going through a midlife crisis? Is there a new sports car to support that one? Struggling through the anguished questions of "how did this happen?" is part of loving someone who's in a dark place. On the other hand, if I read in the paper that some celebrity couple broke up, I'm not going to give much thought to what happened. I'm more likely to shrug at the vagaries of romance in the spotlight, hope it's not too hard on the children, and go back to what I was doing.

Now let's take it back to the more abstract level. If I claim to love my neighbors and those neighbors are suffering, it is my obligation to make some effort to understand why. That is, I need to *see* them, to gaze in their direction long enough to understand. Of course, in these days of advanced globalization, my "neighbor" is everyone in the world. This means that on a practical level, I'm only going to be able to do "analysis" in any depth with so many of them. But if the neighbors on my doorstep say their problems are rooted in racism, for example, then love means that I don't get to dismiss that complaint. Loving them as myself, as I love my best friend, as I claim to love Christ, means I'm not going to brush off their grievance and tell them that if they'd only apply themselves more, they'd be fine. It also means that if my neighbor of the opposing political party is afraid that my party's agenda will destroy the country, I don't get to dismiss them, either.

Cornel West's understanding of love is not a matter of warm feelings; it is fundamentally about taking people seriously, and I'm not doing that if I'm not listening to them and trying to understand their concerns. But analysis without *action* is futile, just as faith without works is dead. West's idea of love is one that cannot stop at the intellectual level, because then it's just a sterile head trip. It's keeping the sort of distance from the real world for which people love to poke fun at academics, though I'm not sure we deserve it more than most people. Again, we can't personally act against every cause of suffering in the world, but love means acting on some of them. This part isn't hard to understand. I think the part that's harder, and that is often skipped over, is analysis. We tend to rush straight from "my neighbor is hurting" to "I must act," without pausing to figure out what's happening and what truly useful action might be. All too often, we assume we know what people need without taking that crucial middle step of listening to them and hearing what they need from us. This has led many a well-intentioned person to paternalistic, "I know what's best for you" acts of charity that often do more harm than good. We unthinkingly fail to approach the other as an equal because we're blind to the *imago Dei*.

These kinds of mistakes happen when we lead from the false self. The false self is primarily motivated not by love but by its own needs: the need to look like a compassionate person, to feel like a good Christian, and even to rack up points with God. The false self wants to look busy and productive, because in our culture that's an important way of getting prestige and esteem. As Rowan Williams observes:

> If we're always tearing around looking busy, thinking of things to do . . . the chances of actually attending to what other people are like and what other people really need get smaller and smaller. We are so concerned to keep ourselves busy that we don't actually stop to ask, "Do people need me to be busy like this?"[5]

Williams goes on to say that prayer is a key part of getting beyond this. When we calm down and open ourselves to others in the presence of God, we will begin to see what their real needs are: "Those people who spend long, long periods in prayer and in silence are, in my experience, the people who respond to you as you really are most effectively, most warmly and quickly."[6]

We not only need to know who we really are; we also need to deal with others as they really are. Both analysis and prayer are important to this. Taking people seriously is a process, one that's just as complex and challenging as preparing to see the face of God. There's a reason for that: we're purifying our hearts so that we can see the face of God in our neighbor. The two journeys are really one, and both of them require that the false self take a beating and ultimately die. Then we will be able to say with St. Paul, "it is no longer I who live, but it is Christ who lives in me. And the life I now live in the flesh I live by faith in the Son of God, who loved me and gave himself for me."[7] When it is Christ who lives in us, then we are able to love others and give ourselves for them. And those streams of living water that Jesus promised flow, unpolluted, to the thirsty people around us.

Authentic Action

Love, in short, begins with right seeing; it takes a steady and persistent gaze to recognize the *imago Dei*, especially where it's most deeply hidden. Love continues through right analysis, the ability to understand people's situations and needs. This often means we need to gaze at suffering, violence, and injustice when we'd rather look away. Finally, love takes us to right action. Once we've seen the worth of others and the urgency of their need, we must act, whether that involves choosing a career or a form of service for our spare time.

But right action requires clear seeing too. Choosing the correct path is tough in the dark; how do we figure out what sort of action to take? People often frame the question in this way: What is God's will for me? How can I discover the divine Plan, so that I can go along with it? But this may be asking the wrong question, or maybe it's asking a reasonable question but not in the most helpful form. It's as if God has a very specific plan all worked out for you, which you must somehow figure out and then force yourself to conform to. Another way to ask the question is this: What action could I take that would respond to the needs I see and be consistent with who I really am? Serving from an authentic identity is important, because doing service that's not really you, that isn't a good fit with who you are, is a quick route to burnout. If you're exhausted by doing the work and keeping up the pretense too, you may end up doing more harm than good. Ministry is about relationships, and relationships need to be real.

We've already touched on how our relationships with others would be different if we led from our true self, and I want to return to that question for just a moment before moving on to talk about the true self and vocation. A lot of those differences have to do with freedom. As our free, true selves, we could make and live with our own choices and meet misunderstanding and disapproval from others with acceptance. Our dealings with others would be less reactive, less driven by old wounds that are torn open anew by criticism, opposition, or control. We'd be able to "speak the truth in love" rather than holding it in or blasting people with it like a blowtorch. We'd also be able to hear truths that others speak to us without being shamed, threatened, or combative, without denying, hiding, or passing the buck. In short, we'd simply "be ourselves," and that does sound simple, doesn't it? But it isn't, really, and sociology helps us understand why.

When I introduce my Survey of Sociology students to dramaturgical analysis and the ways we perform our selves for others, one of the things I ask them is, "Why put all this effort into staging ourselves? Why can't you just 'be yourself'?" (This question is accompanied by a slide that reads, "Always be yourself. Unless you suck.") We bat around possibilities for a while, but it really comes down to the fact that people don't have access to complete information about us, and because they don't, each thing they learn about us exists on its own, without context. That means that if you show up for a job interview in sloppy clothing, the interviewer can't balance these visual cues with the knowledge that you're meticulous about your work. "Sloppy" is what he knows about you. And because people are what social psychologists call "cognitive misers," the prospective employer is not going to expend unnecessary energy exploring your personality and ferreting out reasons to believe that you will be the world's greatest employee. When a stranger—a first date, your fiancé's parents, the judge—is going to have very little data to go on in making an important decision about you, it's essential that the data they do get send the right signals.

We all know this, of course, which is why we dress appropriately, whether for a job interview or our sentencing hearing. In ongoing, close relationships, however, too much attention to self-presentation can create suspicion, and we wonder why the person isn't being authentic and what they're trying to hide. It's expected that the mask will eventually come off, probably bit by bit, and the other will see who we really are. You can't have intimacy with someone who doesn't really know you. You can have sex, a relationship, kids even, but intimacy requires self-disclosure rather than carefully managed self-presentation. And we seek out intimacy because one of the deepest human desires is to be both fully known and fully accepted.

This is hard work, risky and scary. Being honest with another about something that has always been a source of shame takes a lot of faith, and still feels like stepping off a cliff. Trust me, I've done both and they feel exactly alike. It's tempting to go the passive route and just postpone it indefinitely, or else to actively work at becoming someone who will "match" the other in a way that gains their approval. In my twenties I dated a lovely young man I'll call Steve. Steve was an outdoorsy guy, and I suspect he was one of those people who was hyperactive as a kid and never grew out of it. So he first took me rock climbing, but we also went snow camping, mountain biking, cross-country skiing, kayaking, and whatever else he could think of that involved expending a lot of energy outside. All of this would ideally involve lots of other people, as Steve was the consummate extrovert.

We were both in school at the time, putting in long hours during the week. When the weekend came, Steve's idea of relaxing was to drive to the lodge on Mount Rainier, strap on a pair of skis, and head *up* the mountain. Understand that this is a fourteen-thousand-foot volcano, so this could go on for a very long time. At day's end, we'd head back to Seattle and share the experience with friends over a few beers. For me, there were several problems with this: While I started skiing at around age five, I was always taught to point the skis *downhill.* This is a lot less work, which I appreciated because I'm not a naturally athletic or outdoorsy person. I'm also an introvert who doesn't drink beer. So by the time Monday morning rolled around, I was exhausted and resentful. Eventually, I realized that I needed to stop pretending I was someone who'd make the ideal partner for Steve and just throw him back. If I hadn't, I'd have spent the rest of my life climbing frozen waterfalls and probably overdosed on adrenaline before my thirtieth birthday.

My point is this: we must figure out who we really are and then live from that authentic self. Before I began writing this book, I asked a lot of people, including therapists, spiritual directors, people with various kinds of disabilities, and people in a range of occupations, "What do you think it means to live authentically?" Most of them said some version of, "Be yourself." That's part of the answer, but it's not the whole answer. Living authentically does mean being at home in your skin, but not just so that you can go through life in greater comfort, though that's always nice. It's also so that the service you offer the world is not a lie. Most of us have probably known, perhaps even been, the kind of Christian who feels they have to pretend that having a relationship with Christ means that you're always happy. There are those who worry that if Christians don't look happy, no one else will be attracted to the faith.

The problem is that if they do succeed in drawing in people who are looking for happiness, sooner or later those converts are going to find themselves in a tough place and discover that the "happiness guarantee" was false advertising. What then? One type of person will feel inadequate and try to fake it for the sake of others, keeping the deception alive. A different type will just figure it didn't "work" and move on to something else.

Either way, they've been duped, because God is not calling us to "happiness" but to loving service from a place much deeper than that. As Frederick Buechner has said, "The place God calls you to is the place where your deep gladness and the world's deep hunger meet."[8]

Discerning What Action to Take

So how do we figure out what "action" to take in response to the world's need? I love reading the lives of the saints, because they show us how many different ways there are to please God. On the other hand, it's easy to read stories of superhuman sacrifice and think God must be calling me to the very thing I would find the hardest, the thing I dread the most. It's true that some of us are called, like Peter, to let life take us where we don't want to go, and I don't think God's going to allow any of us to spend our whole life in our comfort zone; that's not the best way for growth to happen. But I think Buechner is on to something. If you pass out at the sight of blood, chances are God is not calling you to be a thoracic surgeon. There's an awful lot of blood in people's chests, and you'd be spending your entire career sticking sharp objects into them. People who believe in that kind of vocation often harbor a secret suspicion that their life's work is supposed to be an atonement for their inadequacies. The mistake lies in forgetting that Jesus already atoned for our inadequacies.

What is your deep gladness? Here's another way to ask the question: Who would you be in the world if you knew you were shining like the sun? If at some critical and very public moment in your life the heavens had opened and God had said to all assembled, "This one is my beloved," how would your life be different now? Or put it this way: What kinds of things would you do if God revealed to you that after you die, they're going to put the word "Saint" before your name and give you a day on the calendar, that people are going to write and read your biography and visit the places that have been important to you? If you knew you were that kind of person, what would you be willing and able to do? Is there any reason not to do those things now?

I've been teaching college students for a couple of decades now, and I've seen so many of them wrestle with the questions of what major they should choose and what career they should prepare for. In a sense, they're trying to learn their true name.[9] It's not uncommon for young people to have to strive to hear their name over the names their families are giving them. Several years ago I had a student whose parents were highly successful professionals, immigrants from the Middle East. She was the youngest, and her siblings were all on their way to promising careers. Her parents wanted, expected, even pressured her to become a pharmacist, as that would be a respectable career—not quite a doctor, but well paid and secure. These are often central concerns in immigrant families, and there's good reason for that: parents who have lived through major upheavals want their kids' lives to be as safe as possible. But this young woman lived to paint, and struggled in her science courses. As a result, she had a profound sense of unworthiness and was seriously depressed when I met her. She eventually found her own way, her own name, but it took real courage and perseverance.

Some people are reluctant to get close to God for fear that if they turn their lives over to God, "He'll make me become a missionary and send me to Africa." I'm inclined to think that if God's paying attention to the growth trends in the church, he's much more likely to send Africans to us. Besides, Africa is a big continent of over fifty countries, with some lovely places to live. The sentiment behind "God will send me to Africa" is real enough, though. Remember how scary those prayers of oblation can be? "Lord, I offer myself to you; may your will be done." What if it really is God's will for you to be a thoracic surgeon and spend your life face down and unconscious in people's open chests?

If this is what you're afraid of, then you might need to rethink your image of God. Muslim tradition holds that there are ninety-nine names of God; I'm no expert on Islam, but I checked the list and "Sadist" is not one of them. I'm not saying that God never calls us to action we don't want to take; the story of the prophet Jonah tells us that those kinds of calls sometimes happen. In the course of a lifetime, we all have to do plenty of things that don't come easily or naturally to us, otherwise *kenosis* would never happen. All jobs and all forms of service have their tedious and difficult aspects, and some days are harder than others. But when it comes to ministry, most of the time I think it's our "deep gladness" God wants us to bring to the world's need, because it will do both the world and us more good than if we bring our deep neurosis and fear. Woody Allen is great as an actor and director, but can you really see him as a social worker or a nurse? I think God might have more sense than that.

I had a friend some years ago, an intensive care physician, who was a woman of deep prayer. Her greatest desire was to go somewhere in the developing world and offer her services. She had done this in the past and loved nothing more than to live in a mud hut in a remote village and care for people who would otherwise get no medical attention at all. She finally got a gig in Tanzania, and before she left we had several conversations about it. I was struck by her excitement, and equally struck by how little I envied her. If I were to make a permanent move to somewhere in Africa, I think it'd have to be a place like Cape Town, which is basically the South African version of Seattle: a vibrant, hip city in a beautiful setting with a mild climate and great restaurants. Mud huts are just not my thing.

For a while, I felt guilty about this: What kind of Franciscan can't live in a mud hut? And if I didn't envy my friend's living conditions, I did envy her for having a vocation that was clearly heroic. I figured she didn't have to wonder whether God was pleased with her, as I so often did. But then I looked at my courses, in which I bring hundreds of students a year face-to-face with human suffering in places like sub-Saharan Africa. I realized that going there and meeting people's needs directly is not my call; it doesn't have my name on it. I was not going to be the one who fed, clothed, and tended Jesus in those people in person. Instead, my job was to stay here and make sure he wasn't forgotten. The students in my classes would spend at least some time gazing at people who live with poverty, AIDS, slavery, and genocide. God gives me what I need for that task, for my call; he doesn't give me the graces for someone else's call. And when a student's gazing at human need motivates a change of direction or a new sense of commitment, that is a deep gladness indeed. When I am midwife to a moment like that, I can hear my name in it. I know that I am serving from who I really am.

It didn't happen overnight, though, as I've already confessed. Figuring out what action you're going to take in the world, how you're going to love the world in the name of Christ, is a process. It's not just a matter of being told what task God's assigned to you and then obeying. Obedience is certainly part of it, but remember that "obedience" is fundamentally *listening*. We listen for the name God gives us, for the name that will say something about our gifts. This process involves prayer, but we also learn to hear God's voice in the voices of other people.

All of this requires discernment, however, as the church—both its members and the institution itself—can be wrong about people's vocations. Some people do end up in ministries where they do more harm than good, while others are shut out of ministries where they might have done a great deal of good. Before I submitted my first book (*Following Francis*) to prospective publishers, I asked several people for advice on whether I should move forward with it. Most were encouraging, but one person said I should shelve the project as I was not spiritually ready to write on the subject. I was prepared to take this advice, being only too ready to believe in my own immaturity. But my spiritual director at the time put it in context and urged me to go ahead with the book. My point is that it's important to solicit advice, but discern carefully what you're supposed to do with it. Even Francis, faced with a decision about whether to continue preaching or retire to a hermitage, asked more than one person for counsel.

Barbara Brown Taylor tells a story about how, when she was in seminary, she was seeking to discern the will of God for her life. She used to climb up a fire escape and "pray the way a wolf howls,"[10] inarticulate cries of the soul. She kept asking God what she was supposed to do with her life and finally heard the answer: "Do anything that pleases you," God said, "and belong to me."[11] God apparently hasn't changed much since the days of St. Augustine, whose advice was to "Love God and do what you will." When our action emerges from the intersection of our passion and the world's need, then the love we bring to the world will be real, because it will come from an authentic self.

Active Contemplation, Contemplative Action

The contemplative gaze leads to personal transformation, but it also leads to social action because to see Christ is to love him, and to love him is to want to serve him. Francis of Assisi loved the blessing God gave to Moses and Aaron to pronounce over the people of Israel:

> The Lord bless you and keep you;
> The Lord make his face to shine upon you, and be gracious
> to you;
> The Lord lift up his countenance upon you, and give
> you peace.[12]

I think Francis must have known through experience that one who sees God's face cannot remain indifferent to God's world. To love God is to love what God loves, and Francis understood that as including not only all people but all of creation.

"And all of us, with unveiled faces, seeing the glory of the Lord as though reflected in a mirror, are being transformed into the same image from one degree of glory to another."[13] I keep returning to this verse to emphasize the transformative power of the sacred gaze. But to be transformed into the image of Christ means not only being transfigured. The more we become like Christ, the more we incarnate the love of God in the world, because that's what he did. "Shining like the sun" means radiating light and warmth to a world that needs them to survive. The idea that the goal of contemplation is to generate a private spiritual buzz is not just a mistake; it's a heresy. Look it up under "quietism." Even the most strictly enclosed monks and nuns serve the world by interceding for it in prayer. It's not a stretch to say that our action is a test of the genuineness of our contemplation: "By their fruits you shall know them." If our gazing at Christ doesn't cause us to turn a compassionate gaze at the world, and motivate us to compassionate action, then we need to check on whether it's really Christ we've been gazing at. If we know nothing else about Jesus, we can be certain at least of this: staying aloof from the needs of the world is not his style.

It's striking to me how much time and ink people have spent debating the relative value of contemplation and action over the centuries, pitting Mary and Martha against each other as if they weren't sisters. (Of course sisters squabble. How else would we know they're related?) It's true that Jesus held Mary up as an example to her sister in Luke's gospel, when Martha was fretting over household duties: "Martha, Martha, you are worried and distracted by many things; there is need of only one thing. Mary has chosen the better part, which will not be taken away from her."[14] We tend to forget that in John's gospel, following the death of Lazarus their brother, it is Martha who makes a bold profession of faith in Jesus: "Yes Lord, I believe that you are the Messiah, the Son of God, the one coming into the world."[15] Mary just weeps and rags on Jesus for not showing up earlier, when he might have done some good.

So if we're going to cast Martha as the activist and Mary as the contemplative, we need to remember that there was a time when the activist saw Jesus more clearly. But Teresa of Avila had it right when she presented these two gifts as complementary:

> [B]elieve me, Martha and Mary must work together when they offer the Lord lodging, and must have Him ever with them, and they must not entertain Him badly and give Him nothing to eat. And how can Mary give Him anything, seated as she is at his feet, unless her sister helps her?[16]

Another great mystic, Catherine of Siena, pointed out that contemplation and action are how we live out the commandments to love God and neighbor. As such, both are necessary, and each reinforces the other: "On two feet you must walk My way; on two wings you must fly to heaven." To pit contemplation against action is like trying to choose between inhaling and exhaling. Life requires both.

One last thing. If you're intimidated by the notion of "action," uncertain that you have anything worthwhile to contribute, remember that Jesus first sent his disciples out two by two to preach and to heal long before they were "ready."[17] It seems they still accomplished what he wanted them to, although he did have to caution them not to get too excited about the power they'd been given. So prepare yourself, do your gazing and your analysis, but don't be such a perfectionist about it that you can't do anything until you know everything. Start small if you like. Take Buechner's advice and love your neighbor by seeing your neighbor. It seems like a small step, but it's such an important one and frequently missed. People often don't see each other, even in settings where you'd think they would. Have you ever had someone shake your hand in church, offer you "Peace," and look straight past you as if they're scanning the room for someone more interesting? There was a book published in the early 1970s called *Be Here Now*, and although I haven't read it past the title, I think that alone could be enough to change my life.

While you're waiting to see if God's going to send you to love people in Mozambique, why not work on loving the person in the next pew, across the conference table, or on the other end of the phone? Maybe that won't make you the next Martin Luther King Jr. or Mother Teresa. But as Rowan Williams is fond of saying, "At the Day of Judgment . . . the question will not be about why we failed to be someone else; I shall not be asked why I wasn't Martin Luther King or Mother Teresa, but why I wasn't Rowan Williams."[18] Maybe my contribution feels like a small one, but the truth is that even the greatest among us are so limited that they can only do the part they've been given by the grace of God; they can't do their part and mine too. So my contribution, however humble, is needed. So is yours. As we learn in St. Paul's famous discourse on love, when we offer back to God the gifts we've been given, they can become "the greatest of these," or degenerate into so much racket, "a noisy gong or a clanging cymbal." It is love, and love alone, that makes the difference.

Chapter 10

Conclusion: The Divine Makeover

> *Good religion is always about* seeing *rightly: "The lamp of the body is the eye; if your eye is sound, your whole body will be filled with light," as Jesus says in Matthew 6:22.* How you see is what you see. *And to see rightly is to be able to be fully present—without fear, without bias, and without judgment. It is such hard work for the ego, for the emotions, and for the body, that I think most of us would simply prefer to go to church services.*
>
> —Richard Rohr[1]

Before we finish, I'd like to get in one more confession: While I generally have a very low tolerance for reality TV, I am a huge fan of the show *What Not to Wear*. As with so many American television shows, this one was based on a British series of the same name, but this is probably the only case I've seen where I thought the American version was better.

Each episode begins by introducing a fashion victim who's been nominated by family and friends for a makeover. The audience is shown footage of the subject, nearly always a woman, in clothes that range from dumpy, oversized, and outdated (like the women who are trapped in the 1980s, wearing blazers with giant shoulder pads) to outrageous (the woman in the Navy who wore nothing but skin-tight cat suits when off duty was a particularly memorable example). The hosts give her five thousand dollars and some "rules" for choosing clothing to maximize her assets and cover her flaws. Then they take her shopping and get her hair and makeup done. It ends with the "reveal," in which she models her new look, first for the hosts and then for friends, family, and coworkers.

It's all great fun, and I've learned some things from watching the show, though in the course of its entire ten-year run I lived in fear of being nominated myself. But almost without exception, the women come away with more than a better wardrobe and a new 'do; they have a new confidence, a new sense of self. It's moving to see how few of these women think of themselves as pretty or even reasonably presentable. Asked when the last time was that they felt beautiful, many of them just burst into tears, forced to confront a subject they've been avoiding for years. The hosts take them apart by making them model their own clothes in a 360-degree mirror. They make the subject take a good, honest look at how what she's doing isn't working. And then they spend a few days building her back up—both her look and her confidence. They talk up her accomplishments and tell her that the goal is for the outside to be congruent with the inside, that she should look like the woman she really is.

Wouldn't it be great if there were a spiritual equivalent of this program? They could call it *Who Not to Be,* and take people with a frumpy sense of self through a makeover process that would look honestly at their weaknesses and then play up their strengths. It could end with a "reveal" scene (a transfiguration) in which they'd see that they are actually shining like the sun. Then they'd be exhorted to remember what they've seen, and go out and act like that person.

I suspect that something like this is waiting for us in the life to come. But in the meantime, I don't see any reason why we can't get started now, especially when God is so eager to make us over so that what we and others see is consistent with who we really are. As Ilia Delio has said, "The more we allow ourselves to be transformed by the Spirit of love, the more we become ourselves, and the more we become ourselves, the more we are like God."[2] In this book, I've tried to show something of what that process might look like. Let's take a moment to retrace our steps and get a sense of the journey as a whole.

The Wounding and Healing of the Self

We are indeed shining like the sun, but when most of us look through the eyes of the false self, we see either the glare of self-aggrandizement or the shadow of self-contempt. Because we can't see ourselves directly, we need a mirror, but the images reflected to us by society at large and the individuals in our circle are distorted and untrue. Confused, we ask, "Who am I?" and as long as we keep up the search, each new piece of data that comes in makes us readjust the picture. Even if we come to a settled and fairly positive view of ourselves, disappointment, failure, and loss can shake it loose like an Etch-A-Sketch, and we start all over again.

The world around us is full of mirrors, but it's the people who know us best and love us most who will give us the most accurate view. Even there, however, distortions will come in. Maybe my best friend knows I'm kidding myself about what a good listener I am. Maybe I actually have a bad habit of bringing every conversation around to myself, but she can't figure out a way to tell me that won't hurt my feelings. Or maybe my friend has noticed that I'm such a great listener that people are always seeking me out as a confidante, but she doesn't tell me, out of envy. What I need is someone who both knows and loves me perfectly—infinitely and unconditionally—who is committed to showing me the truth about myself, in love. Someone who's not interested in either flattering or diminishing, but is committed to my transformation and to accompanying me on what Teresa of Avila called the "way of perfection." When I find that Mirror, looking at it every now and then will not be enough. The divine looking glass is not for glancing; it is for gazing.

Gazing takes preparation, however, because the light of God is so powerful. We can't look straight into the face of God, any more than we can look straight at the sun; too much light too soon can destroy our vision altogether. We are going to have to visit some dark places before we're ready for uncreated Light, places where everything we thought we knew about ourselves, and everything we offered the world in our dramatic presentation of ourselves, is emptied out. The deeper this process of *kenosis* goes, the closer we get to the *point vierge*, our deepest, truest self. It is at this level, in this emptied-out space, that we have room to offer hospitality to God. The good news is that God is already there, waiting for us to show up.

That God is committed to my healing and freedom is good news indeed, although God is the only physician I know whose treatment plan begins with death. I love the fact that on *What Not to Wear*, they don't bring in a tailor and alter the subject's current wardrobe, taking out the shoulder pads and restitching the seams. They bring a trash can onto the set and throw it all out, so she can start anew. I also love how the "rules" they give for shopping vary from one subject to the next, because every woman is different. A woman with an hourglass figure crammed into five feet of height is going to get a different set of rules from a woman who's tall and angular.

Likewise, God works with each of us in ways that respect our individuality. The imagination can be a powerful means of cultivating a Godward gaze, but we differ in both the extent and the ways we bring our imagination to prayer. *Gazecraft* includes all kinds of methods, but the goal is the same: to fix our attention on Christ so that we may see our true self reflected in his eyes, and learn the particular way he calls each of us "Beloved." To see ourselves transfigured, and know that this glorified version of us is already real to God, is to experience a deep healing indeed. When we bring that authentic self to others, the self we mirror back to each of them will be loving and true. Then we will be partners with God in bringing healing to a blind and broken world.

The contemplative gaze is not the whole answer to the problem of a fractured self. We need to practice this prayer in the context of other spiritual disciplines: the sacraments, study, spiritual direction, active ministry, and so on. We also need to care for ourselves psychologically and physically, challenge ourselves intellectually, and nurture ourselves emotionally. But a focused gaze on God is vitally important, because there are so many other things competing for our attention, and as long as we allow them to distract us, it will be hard to resist believing in the selves they mirror back at us. As long as we're seduced by those false images, it'll be hard to love God and neighbor, because we'll remain trapped in the service of our own ego.

It's not easy to get past that; at least, it's not proving easy for me. When he was a lot further along the path than I am, Francis of Assisi asked, "Who am I?" and I am still asking. There are days when I have no idea who I am, but this may actually be a good sign. As a human being, the one thing I know about myself for certain is that I'm made in the image of God. Anyone who's ever tried to explain the doctrine of the Trinity knows that there comes a point when you just have to shrug and say, "It's a mystery." The God in whose image we're made is a mystery, so when we mystify ourselves, perhaps we're actually getting a glimpse of the Divine within us. As we gaze into that holy Abyss, we discover that the Abyss gazes back at us. The more we seek to connect to that, to live from the *point vierge*, and to gaze on the One whose habitation it is, the more we will come home to our true self, the glory of God, a human being fully alive.

Notes

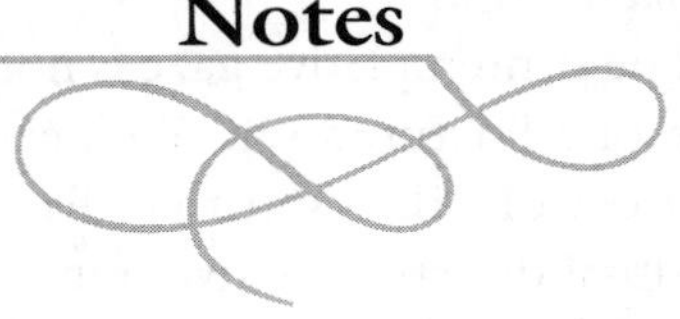

Notes to Preface, pages xi–xiv

1. Ilia Delio, *Franciscan Prayer* (Cincinnati, OH: St. Anthony Messenger, 2004).
2. 2 Pet 1:4 (NKJV).

Notes to Chapter One, pages 1–6

1. Thomas Merton , *Conjectures of a Guilty Bystander*. Quotation taken from http://www.law.louisville.edu/cardinallawyer/node/61; accessed June 27, 2012.
2. 2 Cor 3:18 (NAB).
3. 1 Cor 13:12.
4. Thomas Merton, *New Seeds of Contemplation* (New York: New Directions Books, 1961), 34–35, quoted in: Will Carreras, "Discerning the False Self"; http://iconchurchsandiego.com/2010/08/discerning-the-false-self/; accessed June 28, 2012.
5. Ilia Delio, *Clare of Assisi: A Heart Full of Love* (Cincinnati, OH: St. Anthony Messenger, 2007), 42.
6. Erving Goffman, *The Presentation of Self in Everyday Life* (New York: Anchor, 1959).
7. Matt 7:24-27.
8. Eph 4:22-24.
9. Rev 22:15.
10. Matt 17:2.
11. 1 Thess 4:13.
12. Quoted in John Welch, *The Carmelite Way: An Ancient Path for Today's Pilgrim* (Mahwah, NJ: Paulist Press, 1996), 66; emphasis added.

Notes to Chapter Two, pages 7–20

1. William P. Young, *The Shack: Where Tragedy Confronts Eternity* (Newbury Park, CA: Windblown Media, 2007), 181.

2. Quoted in Claire Marie Ledoux, *Clare of Assisi: Her Spirituality Revealed in Her Letters* (Cincinnati, OH: St. Anthony Messenger, 2003), 91.

3. Ibid., 92, emphasis added.

4. Phil 2:6-8.

5. Emphasis added.

6. Charles Horton Cooley, quoted in Lewis A. Coser, *Masters of Sociological Thought: Ideas in Historical and Social Context* (New York: Harcourt Brace Jovanovich, 1977), 306.

7. 1 John 4:8.

8. Ilia Delio, *Christian Life: An Adventure in Love*, audio CD (Now You Know Media, 2008).

9. Matt 22:37-39.

10. See Elaine Heath, *The Mystic Way of Evangelism: A Contemplative Vision for Christian Outreach* (Grand Rapids, MI: Baker Academic, 2008), chap. 2.

11. Rom 7:15.

12. *The Book of Common Prayer* (New York: Oxford, 1928), 6.

13. Thomas Keating, "Monastic Interreligious Dialogue," *Gethsemani Encounter II* (April 2002); http://76.227.210.78/a.php?id=388&t=p; accessed December 12, 2011.

14. Ibid.

15. 1 Tim 1:15.

16. Matt 16:24-25; John 12:24-26.

17. John 8:32.

18. Thomas Merton, *The New Man*, quoted in M. Basil Pennington, *True Self, False Self: Unmasking the Spirit Within* (New York: Crossroad, 2000), 87–88.

19. Melissa Milkie, "Social Comparisons, Reflected Appraisals, and Mass Media: The Impact of Pervasive Beauty Images on Black and White Girls' Self-Concepts," *Social Psychology Quarterly* 62, no. 2 (June 1999).

20. " Suicide Risk High with Body Image Obsession"; http://www.banderasnews.com/0608/hb-highrisk.htm.

21. "Ryan's Story"; www.ryanpatrickhalligan.org; accessed July 14, 2012.

22. "Megan Meier's Story"; http://www.meganmeierfoundation.org/megansStory.php; accessed July 14, 2012.

23. "'Sexting' Bullying Cited in Teen's Suicide"; http://today.msnbc.msn.com/id/34236377/ns/today-today_news/t/sexting-bullying-cited-teens-suicide/; accessed July 14, 2012.

24. Claude M. Steele, "A Threat in the Air," *American Psychologist* 52, no. 6 (June 1997): 613–29.

25. Edwin M. Lemert, *Social Pathology: Systematic Approaches to the Study of Sociopathic Behavior* (New York: McGraw-Hill, 1951). Allen E. Liska, Perspectives on Deviance (Upper Saddle River, NJ: Prentice Hall, 1987).

26. Erving Goffman, *Stigma: Notes on the Management of Spoiled Identity* (London: Penguin Group, 1990).

27. In Western societies this will be more true of dominant group members than of minority group members, who typically retain a higher degree of communalism since they need solidarity to survive.

28. Rodney Stark, "How New Religions Succeed: A Theoretical Model," in *The Future of New Religious Movements*, ed. David G. Bromley and Phillip E. Hammond (Macon, GA: Mercer University Press, 1987), 13, 19.

29. David Richo, "The Sacred Heart of the World: Restoring Mystical Devotion to Our Spiritual Life," *The Way of St. Francis* 15, no. 1 (January–February 2009): 30.

30. Cf. *The Little Flowers of St. Francis of Assisi*, in *St. Francis of Assisi: Omnibus of Sources*, ed. Marion A. Habig (Quincy, IL: Franciscan Press, 1991), 1146.

31. Rom 8:29.

32. John 14:27.

33. Susan Pitchford, *Following Francis: The Franciscan Way for Everyone* (Harrisburg, PA: Morehouse, 2006); I first encountered this image in Thomas Kelly's classic work *A Testament of Devotion* (San Francisco: HarperSanFrancisco, 1992 [1941]), 35–36.

Notes to Chapter Three, pages 21–37

1. John P. Gorsuch, *An Invitation to the Spiritual Journey* (Mahwah, NJ: Paulist Press, 1990), 30.

2. Job 38:4.

3. Eccl 5:2.

4. Susan R. Pitchford, *God in the Dark: Suffering and Desire in the Spiritual Life* (Collegeville, MN: Liturgical Press, 2011), chap. 6.

5. Some good texts on the problem of evil and suffering include Harold S. Kushner, *When Bad Things Happen to Good People* (Harpswell, ME: Anchor, 2004 [1984]); Louis Evely, *Suffering* (New York: Herder and Herder, 1967); C. S. Lewis, *The Problem of Pain* (New York: Touchstone, 1996); Kerry Walters, *Soul Wilderness: A Desert Spirituality* (Mahwah, NJ: Paulist Press, 2001); and Alan Jones, *Soul Making: The Desert Way of Spirituality* (San Francisco: HarperOne, 1985).

6. Luke 13:1-5.

7. Ps 90:4.

8. Rom 8:18-28.

9. By, for example, Phillip Cary, to whose lecture series *The History of Christian Theology* (The Great Courses, Chantilly, VA: course number 6450, 2008) I am indebted for much of this discussion on the treatment of Christ's identity in the gospels, especially lectures 4 ("The Synoptic Gospels") and 5 ("The Gospel of John").

10. Luke 7:49.

11. Mark 4:41.

12. Luke 9:9.

13. Matt 3:17.

14. Matt 4:1-7.

15. Matt 4:8.

16. Mark 9:7.

17. Mark 9:19.

18. Eph 6:12.

19. John 11:41-42.

20. John 12:9-11.

21. Matt 16:16.

22. Matt 16:17-19.

23. Luke 9; Matt 17.

24. See Exod 3:14.

25. Judaism 101, "The Name of God"; http://www.jewfaq.org/name.htm; accessed November 13, 2012. Thanks to Lev Raphael for drawing my attention to this site and for helping me understand the significance of the Name in Jewish thought.

26. Ibid.

27. Ibid.

28. John 8:12.

29. John 10:7.

30. John 6:48.

31. John 6:28, 29.

32. John 11:25, 26.
33. John 14:6.
34. John 15:1, 4.
35. John 8:24.
36. John 8:58.
37. Cary, op. cit.
38. John 19:11.
39. Isa 42:6.
40. Matt 8:28-34; Mark 5:1-20; Luke 8:26-39. In the analysis that follows, I am greatly indebted to two sermons preached on Luke's account of this healing on June 23, 2013, one by the Rev. Rachel Endicott of Christ Episcopal Church of Seattle, Washington, and the other by the Rev. Karen Haig of St. Thomas Episcopal Church, Medina, Washington. The latter can be heard at the St. Thomas Online Coffee Hour website: http://stthomasonlinecoffeehour.blogspot.com/2013_06_01_archive.html; accessed July 2, 2013.
41. Mark 5:9.
42. Jas 2:19 (KJV).
43. Sermon preached on June 23, 2013: St. Thomas Online Coffee Hour; http://stthomasonlinecoffeehour.blogspot.com/2013_06_01_archive.html; accessed July 2, 2013.
44. You'll be relieved to know that I made it through statistics with a respectable, if not impressive, grade.
45. See Matt 13:9.
46. John 8:32.
47. Thomas Keating, *Invitation to Love: The Way of Christian Contemplation* (London: Bloomsbury, 2011 [1992]).
48. Matt 4.
49. M. Basil Pennington, *True Self, False Self: Unmasking the Spirit Within* (New York: Crossroad, 2000), 33–34.
50. John 8:34, 36.
51. Gal 5:22-23.
52. Apologies to all the real cops, who don't actually sit around eating doughnuts all day.
53. It should be noted that, today, people with Hansen's disease prefer not to be known as "lepers." I'm keeping the language here, however, to locate the story in a specific historical context and to emphasize the stigma long associated with "leprosy."
54. Thomas Merton, *New Seeds of Contemplation*, quoted in M. Basil Pennington, *True Self, False Self*, 85–86.
55. 1 Cor 2:16; Phil 2:5.

Notes to Chapter Four, pages 38–59

1. Rowan Williams, Three Lectures on Narnia, lecture 2: "I Only Tell You Your Own Story"; http://www.faith-theology.com/2011/04/rowan-williams-three-lectures-on-narnia.html; accessed August 29, 2013.

2. "The First Letter to the Blessed Agnes of Prague," The Franciscans; http://www.franciscanfriarstor.com/archive/stfrancis/St_Clare_of_Assisi/stf_st_clare_of_assisi_writings.htm#The First Letter to Blessed Agnes of Prague; accessed July 16, 2013.

3. Ibid.

4. N. M. Heckel, "Sex, Society, and Medieval Woman"; http://www.library.rochester.edu/robbins/sex-society; accessed July 16, 2013.

5. Thomas Merton, *Conjectures of a Guilty Bystander* (New York: Bantam Doubleday Dell, 1994), 158.

6. See, for example, Elizabeth A. Dreyer, *Passionate Spirituality: Hildegard of Bingen and Hadewijch of Brabant* (Mahwah, NJ: Paulist Press, 2005); Saskia Murk-Jansen, *Brides in the Desert: The Spirituality of the Beguines* (London: Darton, Longman and Todd, 1998); and Susan R. Pitchford, *God in the Dark: Suffering and Desire in the Spiritual Life* (Collegeville, MN: Liturgical Press, 2011).

7. Mechthild of Magdeburg, *The Flowing Light of the Godhead*, trans. Frank Tobin (Mahwah, NJ: Paulist Press, 1998), 61–62.

8. Learn the basics about the Myers-Briggs Type Indicator here: "MBTI Basics," The Myers & Briggs Foundation website; http://www.myersbriggs.org/my-mbti-personality-type/mbti-basics/; accessed July 31, 2013.

9. Chester P. Michael and Marie C. Norrisey, *Prayer and Temperament: Different Prayer Forms for Different Personality Types* (Charlottesville, VA: Open Door, 1984), 123.

10. Ibid., 150.

11. 1 Cor 13:6.

12. Westminster Shorter Catechism: http://www.creeds.net/Westminster/shorter_catechism.html; accessed July 19, 2013.

13. Luke 10:42.

14. Isa 43:1.

15. Isa 49:16. If you're inclined to dismiss these as promises to Israel and not to you, I'd invite you to review the New Testament letters to the Romans, Galatians, and Colossians, in which we are assured that the difference between Jew and Gentile are no longer relevant.

16. Rev 2:17.

17. Luke 3:22.

18. John 17:22-23.

19. Rowan Williams, "Staying Spiritually Healthy: Maintaining a Healthy Spiritual Life under Pressure," address at the University of Warwick, May 26, 2012, transcript and audio recording, 27:00, Dr. Rowan Williams 104th Archbishop of Canterbury website; http://rowanwilliams.archbishopofcanterbury.org/articles.php/2512/archbishops-study-morning-university-of-warwick; accessed July 11, 2013.

20. Ibid.

21. Henri Tajfel, *Human Groups and Social Categories: Studies in Social Psychology* (Cambridge: Cambridge University Press, 1981).

22. Scott Kallal's "Discovering Your God-Given Identity" inspired some of Scott Kallal's ideas in his "Discovering Your God-Given Identity," Ezine Articles; http://ezinearticles.com/?Discovering-Your-God-Given-Identity&id=6856990; accessed July 11, 2013.

23. Rowan Williams, "Archbishop Rowan's Sermon at St. Alphege, Seasalter," June 17, 2012, transcript and audio recording, 22:00, Dr. Rowan Williams 104th Archbishop of Canterbury website; http://rowanwilliams.archbishopofcanterbury.org/articles.php/2586/archbishop-rowans-sermon-at-st-alphege-seasalter; accessed July 11, 2013.

24. John 8:34, 36.

25. Thomas Ryan, *Four Steps to Spiritual Freedom* (Mahwah, NJ: Paulist Press, 2003).

26. Thomas Merton, *Seeds of Contemplation* (New York: Dell, 1960 [1949]), 20, 22, quoted in Thomas Ryan, *Four Steps to Spiritual Freedom*, 19.

27. 2 Cor 5:17-18 (MSG).

28. Gal 1:10.

29. Gal 3:1.

30. Gal 4:19-20.

31. Susan Pitchford, *Following Francis: The Franciscan Way for Everyone* (Harrisburg, PA: Morehouse, 2006), chap. 13.

32. Personal communication, June 28, 2013.

33. Ilia Delio, *Clare of Assisi: A Heart Full of Love* (Cincinnati, OH: St. Anthony Messenger, 2007), xxii.

Notes to Chapter Five, pages 60–74

1. Isa 6:5.

2. Isa 6:6-7.
3. Matt 5:8.
4. Matt 5:6.
5. 1 Cor 13:12.
6. 1 Cor 13:9 (KJV).
7. 1 Cor 13:11.
8. A fairly straightforward explanation can be found at "State or Way (Purgative, Illuminative, Unitive)," New Advent; www.newadvent.org/cathen/14254a.htm; accessed October 16, 2013. I have drawn heavily on this website in this section.
9. Undoubtedly this is a process undergone by believers of all faiths, but in this context we're confining ourselves to the mystic ascent in the Christian tradition.
10. Not everyone experiences the unitive state in these terms, that is, as spiritual marriage. Some describe it as "deification"; see Evelyn Underhill, *Mysticism: A Study in Nature and Development of Spiritual Consciousness* (Stillwell, KS: Digireads, 2005 [1911]); also Pitchford, *God in the Dark*, chap. 9.
11. "Bernard of Clairvaux"; http://people.bu.edu/dklepper/RN413/bernard_sermons.html; accessed October 16, 2013.
12. This doesn't mean that we don't love anyone but God. It means that we love others better, less selfishly, because we love them in, through, and for God.
13. Song 1:2.
14. Purists will prefer the designation "Teresa of Jesus."
15. Frustrated readers can turn to Rowan Williams, *Teresa of Avila* (London: Continuum, 1991), which has a very helpful chapter on *The Interior Castle*.
16. Paul Trafford, "Visions Within: Spiritual Development and the Evolution of Imagery in Teresa of Avila's *The Interior Castle*"; http://www.chezpaul.org.uk/chrstian/MSt_essay2.htm; accessed July 17, 2012. I am indebted to Trafford's work, as well as that of Rowan Williams' *Teresa of Avila*, for much of my discussion of Teresa's work.
17. Yes, I know, not that kind of doctor!
18. Teresa of Avila, *The Interior Castle* in *St. Teresa of Avila*, vol. 2, trans. Kieran Kavanaugh and Otilio Rodriguez (Washington, DC: ICS, 1980), 1.1.1, p. 283.
19. Ibid. (1.1.3).
20. John P. Gorsuch, *An Invitation to the Spiritual Journey* (Mahwah, NJ: Paulist Press, 1990), 114–15.

21. C. S. Lewis, *The Chronicles of Narnia: The Last Battle*, First Harper Trophy Edition (New York: HarperTrophy), 176.

22. Rowan Williams, Lectures in Holy Week 2009, Lecture 2: "Reformers, Catholic and Protestant," April 6, 2009, audio recording, 22:00, Dr. Rowan Williams 104th Archbishop of Canterbury website; http://rowanwilliams.archbishopofcanterbury.org/articles.php/815/archbishops-lectures-in-holy-week-2009; accessed August 29, 2013.

23. Trafford, "Visions Within."

24. *The Interior Castle*, 7.4.6, p. 446.

25. For more on the apophatic and kataphatic ways of prayer, see Pitchford, *God in the Dark*; Janet K. Ruffing, RSM, "The World Transfigured: Kataphatic Religious Experience Explored through Qualitative Research Methodology," *Studies in Spirituality* 5 (1995).

26. Thanks to Judith Gillette, TSSF, for drawing my attention to the link between the story of Abba Joseph and the problem of getting stuck in Teresa's third mansion.

27. Christine Valters Paintner, "Becoming Fire," July 31, 2006, Abbey of the Arts: Transformative Living through Contemplative and Expressive Arts website; http://abbeyofthearts.com/blog/2006/07/31/becoming-fire/; accessed June 26, 2012; emphasis added.

28. Brennan Manning, *The Signature of Jesus: The Call to a Life Marked by Holy Passion and Relentless Faith* (Sisters, OR: Multnomah, 1996), chap. 2. Manning is working off the film version, in which Dulcinea plays a more prominent role than in the book.

29. Carl McColman, *The Big Book of Christian Mysticism: The Essential Guide to Contemplative Spirituality* (Charlottesville, VA: Hampton Roads, 2010), 222; emphasis added.

30. Gen 3:8-9.

31. Matt 24:4-5.

32. Again, thanks to Judith Gillette, TSSF, for pointing this out to me.

33. "Catholic Official Convicted in Philadelphia Sex-Abuse Trial," *Seattle Times* (June 22, 2012); http://seattletimes.nwsource.com/html/nationworld/2018505448_priestabuse23.html; accessed June 27, 2012.

34. C. S. Lewis, *God in the Dock* (Grand Rapids, MI: Eerdmans, 1972), 109–10.

35. Susan Pitchford, "Too Catholic (for the Protestants), Too Protestant (for the Catholics)," September 17, 2009; http://www.susanpitchford.com/blog.htm?post=634029; accessed July 17, 2012.

36. Matt 23:23.

Notes to Chapter Six, pages 75–88

1. Parts of this chapter are based on presentations made at the Provincial Convocation of the Third Order, Society of St. Francis, Province of the Pacific in Waikanae, New Zealand, October 4–7, 2012.

2. Thomas Merton, quoted at http://bustedhalo.com/dailyjolt/lent-2012-february-22; accessed March 3, 2014.

3. Phil 2:5-8.

4. Luke 14:11.

5. "Gaslighting" is a phenomenon whose name comes from the 1944 film *Gaslight* (originally a play), with Ingrid Bergman and Charles Boyer. A helpful blog post on this pattern can be found at Robin Stern, PhD, "Are You Being Gaslighted?" May 19, 2009, *Psychology Today* website; http://www.psychologytoday.com/blog/power-in-relationships/200905/are-you-being-gaslighted; accessed July 25, 2013.

6. Ilia Delio, *Franciscan Prayer* (Cincinnati, OH: St. Anthony Messenger, 2004).

7. Thomas R. Kelly, *A Testament of Devotion* (San Francisco: HarperSanFrancisco, 1992 [1941]), 45–46.

8. Ibid., 45.

9. http://etymonline.com/index.php?term=obey; accessed December 23, 2013.

10. Kelly, *A Testament of Devotion*, 91.

11. John 1:38.

12. Kelly, *A Testament of Devotion*, 93.

13. Rowan Williams, *Silence and Honey Cakes: The Wisdom of the Desert* (Oxford: Lion, 2003), 83.

14. Quoted in ibid., 82.

15. *The Rule of Saint Benedict*, ed. Timothy Fry (Collegeville, MN: Liturgical Press, 1981), Prol. 1.

16. Gal 2:19b-20a.

17. Carl McColman, *The Big Book of Christian Mysticism: The Essential Guide to Contemplative Spirituality* (Charlottesville, VA: Hampton Roads, 2010), 161.

Notes to Chapter Seven, pages 89–103

1. J. K. Rowling, *Harry Potter and the Deathly Hallows* (London: Bloomsbury, 2007), 792.

2. Pam Parkinson, "Is There a Neurochemical Basis for Falling in Love?" *The Science Creative Quarterly* 6 (2013); http://www.scq

.ubc.ca/is-there-a-neurochemical-basis-for-falling-in-love/; accessed August 1, 2013.

3. Dan J. Stein and Bavanisha Vythilingum, "Love and Attachment: The Psychobiology of Social Bonding," *CNS Spectrums* 14, no. 5 (May 2009): 240.

4. Marnia Robinson, "The Lazy Way to Stay in Love: Steer Your Limbic System to Sustain Romance," *Psychology Today* blog, 2009; http://www.psychologytoday.com/blog/cupids-poisoned-arrow/200909/the-lazy-way-stay-in-love; accessed August 1, 2013.

5. David Benner, "Meditation and the Brain," Serendip website; http://serendip.brynmawr.edu/bb/neuro/neuro99/web2/Benner.html; accessed August 1, 2013.

6. Friedrich Nietzsche, "Apophthegms and Interludes," in *Beyond Good and Evil*, trans. Helen Zimmern (1966), no. 146; http://www.authorama.com/beyond-good-and-evil-5.html; accessed December 23, 2013.

7. John Urry, *The Tourist Gaze: Leisure and Travel in Contemporary Societies* (London: Sage, 1990).

8. Num 21:1-9.

9. John 3:14-15.

10. John 6:51.

11. Ps 34:8.

12. 1 John 3:2.

13. 1 John 4:1.

14. 2 Cor 11:14.

15. Martin L. Smith, *The Word Is Very Near You: A Guide to Praying with Scripture* (Cambridge, MA: Cowley, 1989), 133.

16. 1 John 3:17.

17. Matt 7:16.

18. These are the classic "fruits of the Spirit" listed in Gal 5:22-23.

19. Karen Kuchan, *Visio Divina: A New Prayer Practice for Encounters with God* (New York: Crossroad, 2005), 43.

20. Acts 2:21; Rom 10:13.

21. John 10:27.

22. Jas 1:5.

23. Tanya Luhrmann, "Why Women Hear God More Than Men Do," *Christianity Today* (May 7, 2012); http://www.christianitytoday.com/ct/2012/mayweb-only/why-women-hear-god.html; accessed July 11, 2013.

24. Ibid.

25. Ibid.

26. Chester P. Michael and Marie C. Norrisey, *Prayer and Temperament: Different Prayer Forms for Different Personality Types* (Charlottesville, VA: The Open Door, 1984). Thanks to Teresa Di Biase for bringing this useful book to my attention.

27. Ibid., 49.

28. Ibid., 70–74.

29. Ibid., 75.

30. My discussion of the forms of the imagination is informed by Mary Rose Bumpus, RSM, "The Hopeful Imagination: A Place God Comes to Meet Us," *Presence* 16, no. 1 (March 2010): 24–31.

31. Ps 139:14.

Notes to Chapter Eight, pages 104–23

1. Ilia Delio, *Clare of Assisi: A Heart Full of Love* (Cincinnati, OH: St. Anthony Messenger, 2007), 56–57.

2. Thomas Keating, *Open Mind, Open Heart: The Contemplative Dimension of the Gospel* (New York: Continuum, 1997), chap. 3.

3. This description of *lectio divina* draws heavily on that of Fr. Luke Dysinger, OSB, found at www.valyermo.com/id-art.html (accessed December 16, 2011), which is well worth reading in full.

4. Isa 55:11.

5. John 10:27.

6. Karen Kuchan, *Visio Divina: A New Prayer Practice for Encounters with God.* (New York: Crossroad, 2005).

7. http://www.audiodivina.com/; http://www.patheos.com/Resources/Additional-Resources/Pray-with-Music-Audio-Divina.html; accessed June 29, 2012.

8. Susan Pitchford, *Following Francis: The Franciscan Way for Everyone* (Harrisburg, PA: Morehouse, 2006), 183.

9. Of course, putting the gospel on film inevitably involves interpretation of the text: What is Jesus' facial expression when he says, "You are of your father the devil"? How does he look at the woman caught in adultery? How do the disciples react when Jesus says, "One of you will betray me"? So there is interpretation in *The Gospel of John* but less than there is, for example, in *Jesus* (with Jeremy Sisto in the title role). In one scene in the latter film, the disciples urge Jesus to speak to the waiting crowd. Looking doubtful, he responds: "Do you think I have anything to say?"

10. Ignatian meditation doesn't require beginning with Scripture either, but it does tend to emphasize it.

11. Ps 46:10.

12. Marc Cohen has recently recorded a lovely cover of "No Matter What" and a collection of other songs from 1971 on his album *Listening Booth*. He's managed to take the 1970s feel out of these songs and make them fresh.

13. Thanks to Valerie Lesniak for this advice.

14. Jer 29:13.

15. Song 5:6.

16. Susan Pitchford, *God in the Dark: Suffering and Desire in the Spiritual Life* (Collegeville, MN: Liturgical Press, 2011).

17. John of the Cross is the most famous of these; his work on the "dark night of the soul" has helped countless people through times of spiritual darkness. More recent works in a similar vein include Alan Jones, *Soul Making: The Desert Way of Spirituality* (New York: HarperOne, 1989); Gerald G. May, *The Dark Night of the Soul: A Psychiatrist Explores the Connection between Darkness and Spiritual Growth* (San Francisco: HarperSanFrancisco, 2004); and John Welch, *The Carmelite Way: An Ancient Path for Today's Pilgrim* (Mahwah, NJ: Paulist Press, 1996).

18. When we find ourselves in darkness, it is more important than ever to get help with discerning what's happening. It may be a "dark night of the soul," in which case the answer is indeed to wait in quiet trust. But if it's clinical depression, the answer will be therapy, possibly including medication. If we're out of sorts because of a conflicted relationship, then some form of mediation may be the answer. If we're not feeling vaguely unworthy but definitely guilty over something specific that we know needs to change, then we need confession, forgiveness, and a change of direction.

19. Luke 11:13.

20. Rowan Williams, "The Risen Christ Says, 'In the Depth of This Reality I Will Speak, I Will Be Present, and I Will Transform,'" sermon, October 7, 2009, Dr. Rowan Williams 104th Archbishop of Canterbury website; http://rowanwilliams.archbishopofcanterbury.org/articles.php/864/archbishop-the-risen-christ-says-in-the-depth-of-this-reality-i-will-speak-i-will-be-present-and-i-w; accessed September 11, 2012.

21. Thanks to Edie Burkhalter for these suggestions.

22. Ps 34:5.

23. John 17:20, 22.

24. 2 Cor 3:18.

25. 1 John 3:2.

26. For the discussion on Orthodox treatments of the transfiguration and our participation in it, I am indebted to Phillip Cary's "His-

tory of Christian Theology," especially lecture 14, "Eastern Orthodox Theology," from The Great Courses series.

27. Matt 17:2.

28. 1 Cor 15:20.

29. 1 Cor 15:42-43.

30. 2 Cor 4:16-18.

31. Eph 3:20.

Notes to Chapter Nine, pages 124–40

1. Frederick Buechner, "Art": http://frederickbuechner.com/page-group/landing/quote/QoD-art; accessed March 3, 2014. Originally published in *Whistling in the Dark: A Doubter's Dictionary* (San Francisco: HarperSanFrancisco, 1993).

2. C. S. Lewis, *The Four Loves* (Fort Washington, PA: Harvest, 1971).

3. Cornel West, *Race Matters* (New York: Vintage, 1994).

4. Cornel West, *Prophetic Reflections: Notes on Race and Power in America* (Monroe, ME: Common Courage Press, 1993).

5. Rowan Williams, "Archbishop Rowan's Sermon at St. Alphege, Seasalter," June 17, 2012, transcript and audio recording, 22:00, Dr. Rowan Williams 104th Archbishop of Canterbury website; http://rowanwilliams.archbishopofcanterbury.org/articles.php/2586/archbishop-rowans-sermon-at-st-alphege-seasalter; accessed July 11, 2013.

6. Ibid.

7. Gal 2:20.

8. Frederick Buechner, *Wishful Thinking; A Theological ABC* (San Francisco: HarperSanFrancisco, 1973), 95.

9. Thanks to Edie Burkhalter for making this connection.

10. Barbara Brown Taylor, *An Altar in the World: A Geography of Faith* (New York: HarperOne, 2009), 110.

11. Ibid.

12. Num 6:24-26.

13. 2 Cor 3:18.

14. Luke 10:41-42.

15. John 27:27.

16. Teresa of Avila, *Interior Castle*, trans. E. Allison Peers (New York: Image Books, 1989), 7.4, p. 231.

17. Thomas Keating, *Invitation to Love: The Way of Christian Contemplation*, 20th anniversary ed. (London: Bloomsbury, 2012), 151.

18. Rowan Williams, *Silence and Honey Cakes: The Wisdom of the Desert* (Oxford: Lion, 2003), 95.

Notes to Chapter Ten, pages 141–45

1. Richard Rohr, *The Naked Now: Learning to See as the Mystics See* (New York: Crossroad, 2009), 63.

2. Ilia Delio, *Clare of Assisi: A Heart Full of Love* (Cincinnati, OH: St. Anthony Messenger, 1993), 61.

Index

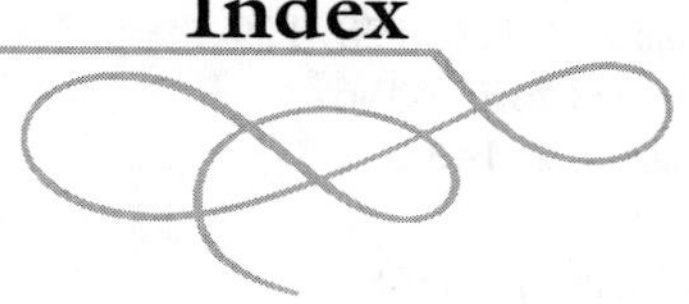